COZUMEL
SURVIVAL
MANUAL

RIC HAJOVSKY

CZM, S. de R. L. de C. V.
P. O. Box 1
Cozumel, Quintana Roo, México 77600

DEDICATION

To the best partner I could ever imagine;
my wife, Marie-France Lemire.

CONTENTS

Introduction

Thinking about moving to Cozumel? Already live here, but are having problems figuring out the system? Either way, this is the book for you. Our island has been attracting Americans ever since 1837 when the Navy of the Republic of Texas raised its flag over the island in Texas' first attempt to annex Cozumel. From the early colonizing schemes attempted by folks like George Fisher (1841), Texan President Sam Houston (1842), Abraham Lincoln (1862) and land promoters like Claude Goodrich (1874), all the way through to the present time-share and condominium ownership plans of today, Americans have flocked to Cozumel in their search for a new life in paradise.

The islanders have always welcomed newcomers and go out of their way to make allowances for people who do not understand Cozumel's laws and customs, but to really get the best out of living here you must try to learn the rules, if not the language. This book is designed to help you learn what you need to know to live happily on our island and avoid many of the common pitfalls that seem to trip-up many new arrivals. You should also check out our webpage **www.EverythingCozumel.com** for lots more tips about living on the island.

¡Benvenidos!

Chapter 1
IMPORTANT PHONE NUMBERS

General Emergency number (ambulance, police, & fire department):
The equivalent to the US 911 emergency number in Cozumel is **066**, but you can also dial **911** and it goes to the same operator

To call for an emergency ambulance only:
For an ambulance, call the Red Cross (*Cruz Roja,* they handle the public ambulance system) at **065** or **872-1058**

FIRE

For the Fire Department *(Bomberos)* **872-0800**
Gas leak detection **872-5759** (Z-gas) and press 9 to report the leak

POLICE

Municipal Police *(Policía Municipal)* non-emergency number 872-0409

Civil Protection *(Protección Civil)* 872-6452

State Police *(Policía Judicial del Estado)* 983-835 0050 ext 1100

Naval Police *(Sector Naval)* 872 5576 (to report narco-traffic activity)

Federal Police *(Policía Judicial Federal)* 872-1777

Public Security *(Seguridad Publica)* 872-0092

Tourist Security *(Seguridad Turistica)* 872-0409

Traffic police *(Tránsito)* 872-0409

GOVERNMENT NUMBERS

Green Angels *(Angeles Verdes)* 078 press 2 for English than 1 for road service

Consumer protection Agency *(PROFECO)* 800-468-8722

Anonymous complaints to City Government 089 from land line

Port Captain *(Capitanía del Puerto)* 872-2409 and 872-0169

Urban Development and Environmental Protection *(Dirección de Desarrollo Urbano y Ecología)* 872-9800 ext 3314

Environment *(Medioambiente)* 872-5795

Public Works *(Obras Publica)* 872-9800 ext. 3298

Electric company *(CFE)* 071 (answered 24 hours a day, Spanish only)

City water *(CAPA)* 872-0391 ext. 112 (Spanish only)

Garbage collection *(PASA)* 869-1900

Airport 872-2081 and 872-0485

HOSPITALS & CLINICS

Red Cross *(Cruz Roja)* office 869-0698

Red Cross *(Cruz Roja)* emergency numbers are **065** or 872-1058

IMSS (social security hospital) 872-0611

Hospital General de Cozumel 872-0525

IslaMed 869-6171

International Hospital 872-1430

Centro Medico Cozumel COSTAMED (CMC) 872-9400

Centro de Salud & recompression chamber 872-0525

BMM hyperbaric chamber 872-1430

Cozumel Hyperbaric Chamber 872-3070

Divers Alert Network (DAN) 001-919-684-9111

Medica San Miguel 872-0103 offices, 872-6104 emergency

TAXIS

987-872-0041 or 987-872-0236

Chapter 2
2017 CALENDAR

JANUARY 2017

1 *Año Nuevo* / New Year's Day (Federal Holiday)

6 *Día de los Santos Reyes* / Three Kings' Day

FEBRUARY 2017

1 (1st Monday observed) *Día de la Constitucion* /Constitution Day (Fed. Holiday)

6 (actual) *Día de la Constitucion* /Constitution Day

14 Saint Valentine's day

19 *Día del Ejercito* or *Día da la Lealtad* /Army Day or Loyalty Day

24 Flag Day (Federal Holiday)

25 & 26 Cozumel Carnaval Parades

28 *Mardi Gras* / Fat Tuesday

MARCH 2017

1 *Miércoles de Ceniza* / Ash Wednesday

1 Burning of Juan Carnaval officially ends Carnaval

19 (celebrated 3rd Monday) Benito Juaréz birthday (Fed. Holiday)

20 Vernal Equinox

21 Benito Juaréz birthday

APRIL 2017

9 *Domingo de Ramos* / Palm Sunday (Holy Week starts)

14 *Viernes Santo* / Good Friday

15 *Sabado de Gloria* / Holy Saturday

16 *Domingo de Pascua* / Easter Sunday

16-17 Cozumel Air Show at Aerodrome

21 *Heroica Defensa de Veracruz* / Veracruz battle memorial

30 *Día del Niño* / Childrens' Day

MAY 2017

Turtle egg-laying season starts, night-time traffic on east coast is limited.

First week of May Cedral Festival

1 *Primero de Mayo* / Labor Day (Federal Holiday)

3 *Día de Santa Cruz* / Holy Cross day (Cedral's special day)

5 *Cinco de Mayo* / May 5th Battle of Puebla (Federal Holiday)

8 Birthday of Miguel Hidalgo, the father of Mexican Independence

10 *Día de las Madres* / Mothers' day

13-15 *Rodeo de Lanchas Mexicanas* (Fishing Tournament)

JUNE 2017

1 *Día de la Marina* / Navy Day (Federal Holiday)

19 *Día de los Padres* / Fathers' Day

20 Summer Solstice

SEPTEMBER 2017

13 *Día de los Niños Heroes* (day honoring the defenders of Chapultepec)

15 The *"Grito"* or call to independence, celebrated at 11 PM at City Hall

16 *Día de la Independencia* / Independence Day (Federal Holiday)

21 *Fiesta de San Miguel* begins (patron saint of Cozumel)

22 Autumnal Equinox

27 *Consumación de la Independencia,* end of the War of Independence

29 Feast of San Miguel ends the Fiesta with a procession to the sea

30 Birthday of Jose Maria Morelos

OCTOBER 2017

12 *Día de la Raza* / Columbus Day (Federal Holiday)

NOVEMBER 2017

1 *Día de los Santos* / All Saints Day

2 *Día de los Muertos* / Day of the Dead (All Souls Day)

19 (3rd Monday) *Día de la Revolución*/Mex. Revolution (Fed. Holiday)

DECEMBER 2017

1-12 *Festival de Guadalupe*

12 *Día de la Virgen de Guadalupe*

13 Hanukkah starts (ends Dec 20)

16-24 Las Posadas (kids caroling *La Rama* for tips)

21 Winter solstice

24 *Noche Buena* / Christmas Eve

25 *Navidad* / Christmas (Federal Holiday)

Puentes, or long weekends
When a federal holiday falls on a Saturday, Sunday, the preceding Friday or the following Monday may be taken off, instead. If the federal holiday falls on a Thursday or Tuesday, the Friday after the holiday or the Monday before the holiday may be taken as well. This four-day weekend is called a *puente*. A holiday in Mexico is called a *día feriado*. A working day is called a *día habile*.

Writing the date
In Mexico the date is written differently than in the US. The day goes first, then the month, then the year. For example, December 9, 2017 is written in Mexico as 9/12/2017. Sometimes the month will be shown in Roman Numerals, as in 9/XII/2017.

Even and odd numbered days
Sometime you may see days referred to as *días pares* or *días nones*. *Días nones* are odd numbered days and *días pares* are even numbered days.

Time
Cozumel changed to the Eastern Standard Time (EST) on February 1, 2015 (UTC/GMT -6 hours), the same as Miami and New York. Daylight Saving Time is NO LONGER observed on the island. If you want to set a computer clock to Cozumel time, set it to the time zone shown for Bogota.

Chapter 3
COZUMEL TRADITIONS

Cozumel has a number of traditional fiestas and celebrations that you will want to know about in advance so you won't be caught off guard and miss out on the fun.

Día de su Santo (Your Patron Saint's Day)

In Mexico, it is traditional to congratulate people on the holy day of the saint they were named after; in the past, these *onomásticas* were more important than birthdays.

Día de los Santos Reyes (Three Kings Day)

January 6, the day traditionally celebrated as the day the three wise men came to Bethlehem, is the day to open your Christmas presents here in Mexico rather than Christmas.

Carnaval

The biggest celebration on Cozumel is without a doubt Carnaval, the wild celebration before the start of Lent. The dates are subject to the Roman Catholic calendar, so they change each year, depending on when Lent begins. Unlike Rio's Carnaval or New Orleans' Mardi Gras, Cozumel's event is very family oriented and inclusive. The carnaval holidays include several weeks leading up to the main events, with private, ticketed affairs as well as free, public events in the plaza and at Parque Quintana Roo, where candidates for the Adult, Teen, and Kid's Kings and Queens of Carnaval are presented and voted into office. Dance competitions between *comparsas* (neighborhood dance groups in home-made costumes) will take place and the city streets will be in a lively state of chaos as these dance groups periodically block off streets and hold impromptu dance parties all over town. The culmination of the celebration are the Carnaval Parades held on the *malecon,* each one full of marching bands and home-made floats, and held over two nights, just so EVERYONE gets a chance to see and celebrate. The last event of Carnaval is the burning of "Juan Carnaval" in effigy, on the night of Ash Wednesday, the beginning of Lent.

Semana Santa (Easter Week)

The week leading up to Easter is the time Mexicans take vacations to visit family or travel to the beach. Consequently, the roads on the mainland are crowded and hotels most everywhere are full.

Feria de Cedral

This fair is held in conjunction with the celebration of the Holy Day of the Cross, May 3rd, the day that Cozumel was first encountered by the Spanish. The dance of the Boars' Head is an integral part of this celebration and is not to be missed. The fair is similar to a county fair in the states, but with the addition of bullfights!

The Sacred Mayan Canoe Journey

This is a new tradition, begun in 2007, which recreates a mythological pilgrimage to Cozumel by canoe from the mainland port of Xcaret. Twenty-five or so dugout canoes are paddled from the mainland to the island by volunteers.

Día De La Independencia and *"El Grito"*

Mexico's Independence from Spain, called for by Miguel Hidalgo in 1810 with his *grito* (shout) of "Down with bad government!" is celebrated in the annual reenactment at City Hall every September 15 at 11 PM followed by fireworks and festivities. The following day, September 16, an independence-day parade marches down the *malecón*.

Festival de San Miguel Arcángel

The holy day of the patron saint of Cozumel is celebrated with processions and food and craft fairs, starting on September 21. The week-long event ends when the Saint Michael statue is taken from the church downtown and carried on a boat surrounded by other boatloads of celebrants throwing flowers into the sea.

Día de los Inocentes and *Día de los Muertos* (Day of the Innocents and Day of the Dead)

On November 1, Cozumeleños remember their deceased children and infants with visits to the cemetery, the building of elaborate family altars, and traditional treats, like *pan de muerto* (dead-man's bread) and *Calaveras de azúcar* (tiny sugar skulls that are labeled with your own name). Another must-have here in the peninsula is the traditional serving of *mucipollo* (it means "buried chicken" in Mayan, referring to chicken that has been baked in an earthen oven) which is a family-sized, chicken tamale that has been baked and not steamed. The following day, November 2, is when all the rest of the deceased adult family members are remembered, often with poems written by their family.

Día de la Virgen de Guadalupe

Starting on December 1 with a religious procession, the event lasts a week with fairs, dances, *mariachi* music, and a race around the island on December 11.

Las Posadas and caroling *"La Rama"*

Beginning December 16 and extending through January 6, Cozumel kids celebrate the journey of Mary and Joseph to Bethlehem. The kids will carry decorated tree boughs and sing carols *(cantando la rama)* for tips and treats all over town during these 9 days.

April Fool's Day comes in December in Mexico!

December 28, *Día de los Santos Inocentes,* is the day Mexico celebrates as a day of tricks and pranks. Traditionally, if someone is foolish enough to loan someone else a small amount of money on this day, the one receiving the money will quickly point out what day it is and say the words *"Inocente Palomita, que te dejaste engañar, sabiendo que en este día, nada se debe prestar."* The meaning in English is: "Innocent little dove, you have let yourself be fooled; knowing that on this day you should lend nothing!"

Friday the 13th is *Martes 13* (Tuesday the 13th) in Mexico!
The combination of date and day of the week considered unlucky in Mexico is Tuesday the 13th, not Friday the 13th as it is in the US and Canada. The popular movie "Friday the Thirteenth" was even re-titled *"Martes 13"* for its Mexican release!

TRADITIONAL ANNUAL SPORTING EVENTS

Annual Kiteboarding and Windsurfing Tournament
For more information, see: **www.cozumelkiteboarding.com**

Rodeo de Lanchas Mexicanas
The Mexican fishing tournament held in May. Your boat must be registered in Mexico to compete. For more information, see:
http://www.pescandoenelcaribe.com/cozumel.html

Annual International Cozumel Island Golf Tournament
Held in May.

ANNUAL EVENTS IN NATURE

Great Land Crab Migration
In late summer thousands of Great Land Crabs (*Cardisoma guanhumi*, a large, blue land crab that spends its mature period ashore) migrate to the sea to lay their eggs.

Marine Turtle Egg-laying Season
Sea turtles lay their eggs in nests they dig in the beach sand here during June, July, and August. The hatchlings crawl out of the nests from November to December. The road on the eastern side of the island is closed to casual night-time traffic during these periods.

Whale Shark Migration Passes by Holbox
July and August are the best months to get a chance to swim with the whale sharks off the north coast of Yucatan during their annual migration.

Chapter 4
THE ISLAND

Geographical and geopolitical location

Located at 20.50529 North latitude and 86.947296 West longitude, the island of Cozumel is 39 kilometers (24 ¼ miles) long by 12.8 Km (8 miles) wide. It lies 20 kilometers (12 miles) from the mainland. The population of over 79,000 is found mainly within its largest town, San Miguel. The only other town on the island is Cedral. Both towns (in fact, the entire island plus two small sections of land on the mainland: the port of Calica with its limestone quarry and the Xel-ha Eco-park) are part of the *Municipio of Cozumel*, a political division rather like a county in the US. The *Municipio* of Cozumel is part of the *Estado* (state) of Quintana Roo, one of the two newest states in Mexico, having been upgraded from a territory along with Baja California Sur in 1974. The state was named after Andrés Quintana Roo (1787–1851), an early patriot of the Mexican Republic. The three *estados* of Campeche, Yucatan, and Quintana Roo together make up the Yucatan Peninsula.

Weather

Cozumel is warm year round, ranging from a rare low of high-60s Fahrenheit in February to the upper-90s Fahrenheit in August. Humidity is high year-round. Water temperature averages around 80 degrees Fahrenheit, climbing to 84 in the summer and dropping to around 78 in the winter. The average rainfall is 63 inches, with the wettest parts of the year being the months of June and September. The driest month is March, followed closely by December. Hurricane season runs from June 1 through November 30. "Tourist Season" runs from December through March, when most Americans and Canadians are fleeing the cold. *Nortes* (north winds) pass over Cozumel with a certain frequency November through December, cooling the island and causing the normally calm water on the western side to become rough and the normally rough eastern side to become calm. The second day of a *norte* is usually ideal for swimming and snorkeling on the "other side" of the island, as the eastern side is often called.

Colonias, fraccionamientos, and parroquias

The city of San Miguel de Cozumel is divided into various neighborhoods, called *colonias*. The term *colonia* is the official designation of a municipal-government delineated residential or mixed-use area and has a recognized border.

There are also neighborhoods that are called *fraccionamientos* (subdivisions) or areas of land that have been sub-divided into residential lots by a developer and sold off one by one to homeowners. *Fraccionamientos* may or may not lie within a *colonia*, but their borders never overlap. If a *fraccionamiento* is built outside of the borders of any *colonia*, it will most likely be re-designated as a *colonia* itself sometime in the future.

A few of the *colonias* in Cozumel were built up in sections, such as San Gervasio 1 and 2, or Flamingos 1 and 2. Most of the time, the sections of the *colonia* developed later are merged with the earlier section to become one combined *colonia*, and the original 1 and 2 suffixes are no longer official. However, in the case of the *colonias* of San Miguel 1 and San Miguel 2, the two sections became independent *colonias*, with the *fraccionamientos* of San Miguel 3 and the *fraccionamiento* of Flores Magon 3 (not to be confused with the *colonia* of Flores Magon located farther to the north east) incorporated into San Miguel 2.

Other geographic place names have also been superseded by newer names over the years, but the older names continue to be used by locals. The name of the *colonia* Gonzalo Guerrero was changed to Colonia Andres Quintana Roo, but nowadays you can see them both used interchangeably in daily use.

Zonas are the commercial equivalent of a *colonia*. On Cozumel, there are the Zona Hotelera Norte, Zona Hotelera Sur, and Zona Industrial.

Another type of geographical division in the city is the *parroquia*, or parish. This ecclesiastically named area is always centered around a

Catholic church. In Cozumel, the area commonly called "Corpus Cristi" is actually the *parroquia* of Corpus Christi, which covers the *colonia* of Andres Quintana Roo as well as parts of the surrounding *colonias.*

Zip codes

Some time back, the city placed a new type of oval street sign at many of the town's intersections. These new signs show the street name, the direction of traffic flow (as indicated by arrows), the zip code *(codigo postal)* and the name of the *colonia* where the sign is located. The problem with the signs, though, is that there was some miscommunication between the department of the government that erected the signs and the post office, so in some cases the zip codes printed on the signs do not coincide with the zip code the post office recognizes as the one for that *colonia.* The list of zip codes contained in the section entitled **MAIL & DELIVERY SERVICES** is the official *Correos de Mexico* list of the *codigo postales* and their corresponding *colonias.* Some c*olonias* have their own zip code and others share a zip code with one or more other *colonias.*

Street names

The mislabeled street signs are not the only misleading directions you will run across here on the island. Many streets and avenues that were once indicated by a numeric designation have had that designation changed by the *Ayuntamiento* to a name to honor a person or a famous place, or a date to honor an historical event. Avenue 30 became Avenue Pedro Joaquín Coldwell. Avenue 65 became Avenida 8 de Octubre. Calle 11 Sur became Avenida Andrés Quintana Roo. Calle 15 Sur became Avenida Xelha. These last two changes broke the old, long standing rule that avenues *(avenidas)* ran north-south and had the right-of-way while streets *(calles)* ran east-west and had stop signs. Some of these new names may make you sound like a time traveler (as in "I live on 8 de Octubre, in the Colonia of 10 de Abril"), however, these name changes (and many other examples of street name changes not mentioned) are often ignored by locals, who continue to use the old numeric designations of streets when giving directions.

As the city grew, the newer sections were often plated and built as unconnected *fraccionamientos* and only later tied into the city's network of streets and avenues, sometimes with odd results. If you travel south on

Calle 90 Sur in Colonia Flamingos, the street becomes Calle 85 Sur at the intersection of Avenida 35, as you pass into the Colonia Taxistas. Traveling south on 8 de Octubre, at one point the streets on the right are numbered (in this mind-numbing order) "23, 1, 25, 5, 27, 13, 31, and 35."

The city also made liberal use of the Spanish word *"bis"* (meaning "repeated") when naming streets. There are many examples of a street having a number designation like Avenida 10 (10th Avenue), only to have the next street over named Avenida 10 bis (10th Avenue Repeated). This to the extreme in Colonia Repobladores de 1848 where you can find an extension of the numeric name to cover more than one street is carried Calle 3 sur, next to a Calle 3 Sur A, next to a Calle 3 Sur Bis.

Some streets and roads have no signs, but do have official names. The coastal road on the west side of the island heading south from the city is the Carretera Costera Sur. The coastal road on the west side of the island heading north from the city is called Carretera San Juan. The section of Avenida Rafael E. Melgar that lies in front of downtown is also called the *malecón* in Spanish (the sea-wall street). Calle Juarez changes name to Carretera Transversal past the eastern edge of town. The coastal road on the eastern side of the island is a federal highway designated C-1 (for Cozumel 1).

There are also the "old" highways; the narrow, two-lane sections of the old *carreteras* that were bypassed when the new, wider sections were laid down. These old sections have special rules. The old highway on the east coast is for bikes and runners only; no cars or motos allowed. Certain sections of the old highway south of El President Hotel are one way south for cars and other sections of it are designated "bicycles only." This usually results in total confusion, with cars, motos and bikes going in all directions because the tourist drivers are oblivious to the poor signage and often drive the wrong way, or drive on the bike paths with motorized vehicles.

Colonias of Cozumel

The map on the following page shows the *colonias* and *zonas* of Cozumel. The area known as Corpus Cristi is actually a *paroquia* (parish) of the Catholic Church and not a *colonia*.

1. Centro
2. 10 de Abril
3. Emiliano Zapata
4. Adolfo Lopez Mateos
5. Cuzamil (INVIQROO)
6. Flores Magon (INVIQROO)
7. Repobladores de 1848
8. Chen Tuk
9. Juan Bautista De la Vega
10. San Gervasio 1 &2
11. Maravilla
12. Indepencia
13. Andres Quintana Roo
    (formerly Gonzalo Guerrero)
14. San Miguel 1
15. San Miguel 2
16. Flamingos 1 &2
17. Taxistas
18. C.T.M.
19. Zona Industrial

20. Huertas Familiares
21. Colonos Cuzamil
22. Zona Hotel Sur
23. Zona Hotel Norte
24. Felix Gonzalez Canto
25. Magisterio
26. Ixchel
27. FOVISSSTE
28. Cozumel Turistico
29. Naval
30. Golondrinas 1 &2
31. Base Area

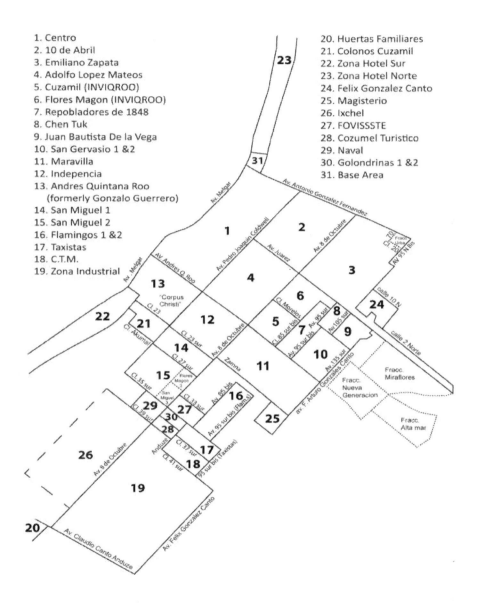

Chapter 5
GOVERNMENT

Local government

The *Ayuntamiento*, or Municipal Government, is run by the *Presidente Municipal* (currently Perla Cecilia Tun Pech, who took office in 2016 and will serve an abbreviated two year term) and the *Honorable Cabildo* (city council), all of whom may not serve back-to-back terms. The city council is made up of a *Síndico Municipal* (municipal trustee), six *Regidores* (aldermen) elected by a simple majority, and three *Regidores* elected by proportional representation along with one *suplente* (alternate) for the *Síndico* as well as one for each of the *regidores*. The Secretaries, Directorates, and Commissions of the *Ayuntamiento* are:

Unidad del Vocero (Spokesperson)
Secretaría General (General secretary)
Oficialía del Registro Civil (Civil Registrar)
Dirección de Bibliotecas Públicas (Public Library)
Secretaría Técnica (Technical Secretary)
Tesorería (Treasury)
Dirección de Contabilidad Municipal (Accounting)
Dirección de Ingresos (Revenue)
Dirección de Egresos (Expense)
Dirección de Catastro Municipal (Land Office)
Dirección de Sistemas (System Management)
Dirección de Fiscalización y Rezago (Audit & Surplus)
Contraloría Municipal (City Controller)
Transparencia y Acceso a Información Pública (Transparency and Public Information)
Oficialía Mayor (Senior Official)
Dirección de Operación y Administración (Operations & Admin.)
Dirección de Eventos (Events)
Dirección de Patrimonio Municipal (City Assets)
Dirección de Recursos Humanos (Human Resources)

Dirección General de Asuntos Jurídicos (Legal Affairs)
Dirección General de Seguridad Pública (Public Security)
Dirección de Tránsito y Transporte (Traffic & Transport)
Dirección de Protección Civil (Civil Protection)
Dirección General de Obras Públicas (Public Works)
Dirección de Comunicación Social (Public Relations)
Dirección de Servicios Públicos (Public Services)
Dirección de Desarrollo Urbano (Urban Development)
Dirección de Desarrollo Social (Social Development)
Dirección de Educación (Education)
Dirección de Cultura (Culture)
Dirección de Deporte (Sports)
Dirección General de Turismo (Tourism)
Dirección de Ecología y Medio Ambiente (Ecology & Environment)
Dirección General de Desarrollo Económico (Economic Development)
Dirección General de DIF (Integral Family Development)
Dirección del Trabajo (Labor)
Dirección de la Juventud (Youth)
Dirección de Equidad de Género (Gender Equality)
Dirección de la Vivienda (Housing)
Planeación Costera y ZOFEMAT (Federal Beach Zone & Coastal Planning)
Administradora Portuaria Integral Municipal (Municipal Port Authority)
Asuntos Internos del Ayuntamiento (Internal Affairs)
Asuntos Internos de Seguridad Pública (Public Security Internal Affairs)
Control Presupuestal (Budget Control)
Dirección de Asuntos Internacionales (International Relations)

State government

Each of Mexico's states has a republican form of government based on the federal system with three branches of government: the Executive branch (a governor and his cabinet), the Legislative branch (a congress, made up of elected deputies), and the Judicial branch (made up of the Superior Tribunal of Justice, an electoral tribunal, and local courts.) Each state is independent and autonomous as far as their internal administration. Cozumel is one of the 10 municipalities that make up the state of Quintana Roo, and lies within the state's *VIII Distrito Electoral Estatal* (the state's Eighth Electoral District). The capital of Quintana Roo is Chetumal. The state governor is Carlos Joaquín González, who assumed office in

September, 2016 for a six-year term. State elected officials cannot serve consecutive terms by law.

Federal government

The United Mexican States *(Estados Unidos Mexicanos)* is a federal republic, made up of 31 states *(estados)* and a Federal District. The Federation is divided into three branches: Executive, Legislative, and Judicial. The Executive branch is headed by a democratically elected president and his cabinet of secretaries. The president, who is both head of state and head of government, is elected for a six-year, non-renewable term as set out by the Mexican Constitution. The Legislative branch is a bicameral congress made up of the Senate and the Chamber of Deputies. The Judicial branch consists of the Supreme Court of Justice of the Nation, the Council of the Federal Judiciary and the collegiate, unitary, and district tribunals. Mexico is a multi-party democracy, but the dominant three parties are: *PAN (Partido de Accion National), PRI (Partido Revolucionario Institucional),* and *PRD (Partido Revolucionario Democratico)*. Cozumel is in the *Primer Distrito Electoral Federal)* First Federal Electoral district.

The Secretariats and Commissions of the Federal government are as follows:

STPS is the Secretary of Labor and Social welfare and oversees labor laws, health and safety.

SEMARNAT is the Secretary of Environment and oversees laws concerning the Environment.

SAGARPA is the Secretary of Agriculture and Fisheries and oversees laws concerning agriculture, livestock, and fisheries.

SS is the Secretary of Health and oversees laws concerning public health and disabilities.

SCT is the Secretary of Communications and Transportation and oversees public transportation, communications, federal highways, airports, airlines, airport security, and hazardous waste.

SE is the Secretary of Economy and oversees foreign commerce, labeling, maquiladoras, product standards, corporations, partnerships, and foreign investment.

SEGOB is the Secretary of Government and oversees immigration, visas, discrimination, CURP numbers, human rights, and investigates government corruption.

SENER-SECRE is the Secretary of Energy and oversees energy, power plants and natural gas.

SFP is the Secretary of Public Function and oversees bidding on government projects.

SCHP is the Secretary of Finance and Public Credit and oversees customs, import/export laws, finances, economic statistics, and taxes.

SRE is the Secretary of Foreign Relations and oversees dual nationality and naturalization.

SEP is the Secretary of Public Education and oversees copyright law and public education.

IMSS is the Mexican Institute of Social Security and oversees the Mexican social security system.

PROFECO is the Prosecutor for the Protection of the Consumer and enforces consumer protection laws.

PEMEX is in charge of the production and distribution of Mexican petroleum products.

SEMIP is the Secretary of Energy, Mines, and Interstate Industry and oversees these areas plus the nuclear industry.

CAN-CONAGUA is the National Commission of Water Management.

SECTUR is the Secretary of Tourism.

INFONAVIT is the Secretary for Workers' Housing.

SEDENA is the Department of Defense.

SSP is the ministry of Public Security.

SEDESOL is the Department of Housing and Urban Development.

SEMAR is the Department of the Navy.

PGR is the Department of Justice.

The Mexican National Anthem *(Himno Nacional)*

Article 45 of the Law on the National Arms, Flag, and Anthem (*Ley sobre el Escudo, la Bandera y los Himnos Nacionales*) states that those who are watching the national anthem performance must stand at attention (*firmes*) and remove any headgear. Since 1943, the full national anthem consists of the chorus, 1st stanza, 5th stanza, 6th stanza and 10th stanza.

Coro Chorus
Mexicanos, al grito de guerra
Mexicans, at the cry of war,
el acero aprestad y el bridón.
make ready the steel and the bridle,
Y retiemble en sus centros la Tierra,
and the earth trembles at its centers
al sonoro rugir del cañón.
at the resounding cannon roar!
¡Y retiemble en sus centros la Tierra,
and the earth trembles at its centers
al sonoro rugir del cañón!
at the resounding cannon roar!

Estrofa I: First Stanza:
Ciña ¡oh Patria! tus sienes de oliva
Let gird, oh Fatherland, your brow with olive of peace
de la paz el arcángel divino,
by the divine archangel
que en el cielo tu eterno destino
for in heaven your eternal destiny
por el dedo de Dios se escribió.
was written by the finger of God.
Mas si osare un extraño enemigo
But if some enemy outlander dares
profanar con su planta tu suelo,

to profane your ground with his step,
piensa ¡oh Patria querida! que el cielo
think, oh beloved Fatherland, that heaven
un soldado en cada hijo te dio.
has given you a soldier in every son.

Estrofa V: **Fifth Stanza:**

¡Guerra, guerra sin tregua al que intente
War, war without quarter to any who dare
De la patria manchar los blasones!
to tarnish the coat of arms!
¡Guerra, guerra! Los patrios pendones
War, war! Let the national banners
En las olas de sangre empapad.
be soaked in waves of blood.
¡Guerra, guerra! En el monte, en el valle
War, war! In the mountain, in the valley,
Los cañones horrísonos truenen,
let the cannons thunder in horrid unison
Y los ecos sonoros resuenen
and may the sonorous echoes resound
Con las voces de ¡Unión! ¡Libertad!
with cries of Union! Liberty!

Estrofa VI: **Sixth Stanza:**

Antes, patria, que inermes tus hijos
O Fatherland, ere your children, defenseless
Bajo el yugo su cuello dobleguen,
bend their neck beneath the yoke,
Tus campiñas con sangre se rieguen,
may your fields be watered with blood,
Sobre sangre se estampe su pie.
may their foot be printed in blood.
Y tus templos, palacios y torres

And may your temples, palaces and towers
Se derrumben con hórrido estruendo,
collapse with horrid clamor,
Y sus ruinas existan diciendo:
and may their ruins continue on, saying:
De mil héroes la patria aquí fue.
Of a thousand heroes, here the Fatherland began.

Estrofa X: **Tenth Stanza:**
¡Patria¡ ¡Patria! Tus hijos te juran
Fatherland! Fatherland! Your children swear to you
Exhalar en tus aras su aliento,
to breathe their last for your sake,
Si el clarín con su bélico acento
if the bugle with its bellicose accent
los convoca a lidiar con valor.
persuades them to battle with courage.
¡Para ti las guirnaldas de oliva!
For you, olive wreathes!
¡Un recuerdo para ellos de gloria!
A memory for them of glory!
¡Un laurel para ti de victoria!
For you, a laurel of victory!
¡Un sepulcro para ellos de honor!
A tomb for them of honor!

Chapter 6
GOVERNMENT OFFICES
(Most of these offices are not in the *Palacio Municipal*)

PROFECO (Consumer Protection agency) You can email them in English at: **extranjero@profeco.gob.mx** or see the webpage: **http://www.profeco.gob.mx/Servicios/quejas_denun_ingles.asp**

Transparencia y Acceso a la Información Pública (**Transparency and Public Information**) is located on the second floor of the *Palacio Municipal*. These folks can give you an answer to almost any question you can come up with regarding the local government and how it functions.
Department of Tourism is open from 9 AM to 2:30 PM on weekdays and the telephone number is (987) 869-0212. It is upstairs on the plaza in the Plaza del Sol between Calle Juarez and Calle 1.

Tránsito (Traffic department of the Municipal Police) is located on the South side of the *Palacio Municipal*, Tel 872-0409

Ecology and Environment is on Av. 8 de Octubre, next to the cenote park, 872-5795

Parks and Museum Foundation of Cozumel *(FPMCQROO)* is on the corner of Av. Pedro Joaquin Coldwell at Juarez, next door to the gas station. Tel (987) 872-0833-**www.cozumelparks.com**
Email: **mercadotecnia@cozumelparks.org**

Animal Control is on Av. 65 near the cenote park. Phone 872-5795

DIF is on Av. 30 between calles 37 & 39, Col. San Miguel II, (987) 857-2300 **www.facebook.com/DIF-Isla-Cozumel-mx**

www.islacozumel.gob.mx site is still not completely functional as on this guide's publication date.

Port Captain is on Av. Melgar at Av. Antonio Gonzalez Fernandez 872-2409 and 872-0169

Inmigración is on the corner of Av. 15 and Calle 5. **www.inami.gob.mx**

Civil Registrar is on Av. Andres Quintana Roo at the corner of Av. 8 de Octubre in Colonia Independencia. They are open 8 AM to 3 PM, Monday through Friday. Their phone is 872-2295.

Main Police Station is next to the *Palacio Municipal* at Avenida Andres Quintana Roo at Calle Gonzalo Guerrero. Phone (987) 872-0409 satellite stations are scattered around throughout the city, always next door to a city park.

Chapter 7
LAWS

Mexico's system of laws

Mexico's laws are based on *Roman Law* (Civil Law, or Napoleonic Law) and not *Common Law* (English Law) like the US. One difference is that judges are more apt to rule based on their interpretation of the law rather that case law precedents. Another is that there are no punitive damages awarded in Mexican lawsuits, which are very expensive and are rarely filed. One very distinct difference is that in Mexican law you are guilty until proven innocent. Crimes are divided into two categories, similar to misdemeanors and felonies in the US. The serious crimes offer no chance of bail. If you are charged with a serious crime in Mexico, you may end up spending a year or more in jail waiting for your case to be heard. Many crimes that are misdemeanors or even civil offenses in the US (like trespassing) are considered serious crimes in Mexico. Mexico has no death penalty. Mexico does have extradition agreements with both the US and Canada.

Drinking

The legal drinking age is 18 in Mexico. Providing alcohol to a minor (under 18) is illegal and taken very seriously. In Cozumel it is illegal to drink alcoholic beverages on the street. It is also illegal to have an open alcoholic beverage in your vehicle. In Mexico, any amount of alcohol in your bloodstream at the time of an accident or traffic infraction will void your insurance (including policies offered by the car or motor scooter rental company, policies offered by a credit card company, or your personal auto insurance) and you will be held legally responsible for the damages or infraction just as if you had a blood alcohol level of above 0.8, the legal limit.

Alcohol sales

Stores can only sell alcohol between the hours of 9 AM and 9 PM, Monday through Saturday, and from 9 AM to 2 PM on Sunday, without a special permit. You must be 18 years of age to purchase alcohol in Mexico.

Age of consent

The age of consent in Quintana Roo is 18.

Public nudity

Although Mexican federal law does not address nudism on its public beaches directly, a municipal law banning "actions that contradict the principles of moral conduct and good customs" can be used by the police to arrest people that appear nude in public.

Illegal drugs

Although a new law decriminalizes the possession of very small amounts of all major narcotics, (including 5 grams of marijuana, one-half gram of cocaine, 50 milligrams of heroin, 40 milligrams of either ecstasy or crystal methamphetamine, and .015 milligrams of LSD), selling drugs is still illegal. The law clearly states any person dealing narcotics will be sent to prison. However, the law is not clear on what amount of drugs in your possession constitute an amount that would be enough to be considered "possession with the intent to sell," so you still risk prison time if you are caught with any amount of illegal drugs in your possession.

Prescription drugs

Any drug classified as a controlled medicine cannot be purchased in Mexico without a Mexican doctor's written prescription. The doctor must also be a federally registered physician. Purchasing or selling a controlled medicine without a valid prescription is a serious crime.

Firearms

Possession of hand guns of up to .38 caliber (excluding .38 Super, .357 Magnum, and 9mm Parabellum or Luger) is legal with a special permit from *SEDENA (Secretaría de la Defensa Nacional)*. Possession of any firearm (or cartridges or shells for any firearm) without a permit will get you a long prison sentence. Possession of a hand gun of a caliber larger than a .38 is illegal, as is the possession of a machine gun or sub-machine gun. Bolt action or semiautomatic rifles and shotguns of a gauge of less the 12 with a barrel length of over 25 inches are legal with a special permit from *SEDENA*.

Knives

Possession of a concealed knife, of any size, can be illegal under many circumstances in Mexico.

Although not specifically outlawed as defensive weapons, any of these items can be interpreted by the police as an illegal offensive weapon.

Military draft

If you have children by a Mexican citizen, the males must sign up for the Mexican conscription lottery regardless of whether or not they have dual nationality.

Honoring the Mexican National Anthem *(Himno Nacional)*

The Law on the National Arms, Flag, and Anthem (*Ley Sobre el Escudo, la Bandera y los Himnos Nacionales*), states that those who are watching the national anthem performance must stand at attention (*firmes*) and remove any headgear.

Carrying proper identification

It is the law that you carry with you at all times proper identification, including (if you are a foreigner) your passport and visa.

Chapter 8
MARRIAGE & DIVORCE

Getting married in Cozumel

You must be at least 18 years old to get married in Mexico without parental consent. With parental consent, both the bride and the groom must be at least 16 years old. You need not be a resident to get married in Cozumel. If you are not a Mexican citizens, you both will need the original and a copy of your passports (valid for at least six more months), the original and a copy of your visas, a *certificado prenuptial* (provided by a local doctor), four witnesses, (each with valid ID). If the woman getting married (this does not apply to the man) was previously married and divorced, she may not re-marry in Mexico during the first 300 days after the divorce decree was final, unless she has given birth during that 300 day period or she can prove medically she is not pregnant. She will also need her apostiled certificate of divorce. You will need to pick up a marriage application at the *Registro Civil*, located at Av. Andres Quintana Roo at the corner of Av. 8 de Octubre in Colonia Independencia. They are open 8 AM to 3 PM, Monday through Friday. Their phone is 872-2295. Fill the application out, noting whether you want to be married under a joint or separate property agreement. You need to have the paperwork turned in to the registrar no later than two business days prior to the marriage. Payment of the marriage license fee (3,300 pesos) includes the marriage ceremony at the registry office for 500 pesos. For 2,500 pesos, the ceremony can take place at another location of your choice. After the wedding, you should get the marriage certificate translated and apostilled in Mexico. The certificate will then be valid world-wide.

If you are marrying a Mexican citizen, in addition to the above requirements, you will need to get permission from the *Secretaria de Gobernación, Oficina de Migración* to marry a Mexican national. The document is known as a *"Permiso para contraer matrimonio con un nacional."*

Common Law marriage

Quintana Roo recognizes common-law marriage *(concubinato).* This status is automatically established between a man and a woman under certain specific circumstances (and after two years of living together in Q. Roo), and brings with it most of the same rights and obligations as marriage, as well as specific rights to support by a wronged partner.

Same-sex marriages

Although the Mexican Legislative assembly of the *Distrito Federal* (Mexico City) has approved a reform to the *Código Civil* that would approve and recognize same-sex marriages in that city, authorities in Cozumel and the state of Quintana Roo do not recognize nor preform them. However, this may change soon, as a judge in the town of Filipe Carrillo Puerto has chosen to interpret the law differently than most and has called the ban into question.

Divorcing in Cozumel

To get a divorce in Cozumel, one spouse must be a legal resident of Quintana Roo. You will need to present to the *Registro Civil* the apostilled birth certificates of both parties, the apostilled marriage certificate, a medical certificate stating the woman is not pregnant, a sworn statement indicating that there are either no children in the marriage or if there are, they are over 18 years of age, *an acta de desolución de sociedad conyugal* certified by a *notario publico*, proof of your residency in Cozumel for at least the past six months, copy of your visa, copy of your passport, and two Mexican witnesses. It takes about two weeks to be final and the cost is approximately $1,700 pesos, plus the *notario publico's* charges.

Names, surnames and family names

Mexican custom dictates that children are christened with at least one (and often several) given names (first names, or *nombres,* in Spanish) at birth. Many of these given names have corresponding English versions (like Peter for Pedro, John for Juan) but, many do not. Besides at least one *nombre,* a child also is bestowed with his father's family name (the *apellido paternal,* or *primer appellido*) followed by the child's mother's maiden name (*apellido maternal* or *segundo appellido*). These names are carried throughout life. When a woman marries, she is not required to add her husband's *primer apellido* to her name. However, if she does wish to add her husband's *apellido paternal* to her name, it would be placed after her last *apellido* and preceded with the Spanish possessive word *"de,"* as in Señora Maria Luisa Olid Pardo de Chan. In social occasions, this can be shortened to Señora Maria Luisa de Chan. If her husband dies and she still wants to keep his name, the word *"Viuda"* (for "widow" and abbreviated *"Vda."*) will be placed just before the possessive *"de"* as in Señora Maria Luisa Olid Pardo Vda. de Chan. When referring to a person by name, there are several ways the name can be applied. For example, a Señor Jorge Pablo Chan Tzuc may be referred to as Sr. Jorge Chan T., Sr. Jorge Chan, or Sr. Chan. Referring to an individual by only his maternal *apellido* (as in Sr. Jorge Tzuc) usually is looked on as an insult, as it intimates the person is illegitimate.

Many people have a nickname (an *apodo*) in Mexico. Sometimes the name can be that of an animal (as in *Pantera*, or *Oso*), sometimes it can reflect a certain body shape or feature (as in *Flaco, Gordo, or Pecas*), and sometimes it is a recognized diminutive of his or her first name (as in Pancho for Francisco, or Pepe for José).

Titles are very important in Mexican culture. If a person earned a degree in the university, they usually expect it to be used when they are referred to by another person. *Licenciado*, (abbreviated *Lic.*) is a common title, one bestowed on a person licensed in a profession, such as an architect or engineer. When referring to someone very respected in the community, the honorific title *Don* is often used before their first name, as in Don Jorge, or Don Jorge Tzuc.

Chapter 9
POLICE

The police forces in Mexico are divided into two main groups; Preventative *(Policía Preventiva)* and Judicial *(Policía Judicial)*. The *Políca Preventiva* provides the security in towns and cities. They do not investigate crimes. The *Policía Judicial* wield much more power. They are organized into three groups; operations (both undercover and plains-clothes), investigating agents, and forensics.

The *Municipio* of Cozumel maintains a preventative police force called the *Policía Municpal*. They handle the day-to-day security on the island. The *Policía Municipal* of Cozumel also has a task force called the Tourist Police, who are all bilingual English-Spanish and patrol the downtown area of San Miguel. The police station in Cozumel is located next to the *Palacio Municipal* at Avenida Andres Quintana Roo at Calle Gonzalo Guerrero. Phone 872-0409

The State of Quintana Roo fields both a state preventative police force *(Policía Estatal Preventiva)* and a judicial police force (the *Policía Judicial Estatal)*. These two bodies enforce both state and federal laws.

Mexico's Attorney General *(*the *Procuraduría General de la República* or *PGR)* fields another judicial police force, the *AFI (Agencia Federal de Investigaciones)*, equivalent to the FBI in the US. The *AFI* investigates federal crimes including drugs crimes, firearm crimes, kidnapping and other organized crimes. The federal government also has a preventative police force, the *PFP (Policía Federal Preventiva)*. The *PFP* enforce federal laws and works together with the Federal Highway Police, Federal Banking *(Fiscal)* Police, and Federal Immigration Police. In addition to these police forces, Mexico also has several "special forces" that are used in situations of terrorism and to fight organized crime. These are the Emergency Rescue Squad, the Task Force Squad, and the Alfa Force. Unlike the US, Mexico uses its armed forces freely inside its borders to support the preventative police forces. The Navy and Army are frequently tasked with setting up road blocks and inspection points throughout the country, as well as assisting in other police operations.

The contents of this chapter are meant to give a general idea of the immigration processes in Mexico. Attempting the "do-it-yourself" approach without the advice of an experienced lawyer is not recommended. Neither the author, nor the editor, is responsible for the application of the content of this guide without proper legal supervision. Bear in mind Mexican laws can and do change. The interpretation of the regulations by individual immigration officers are very subjective. The following rules may be modified at any time.

Chapter 10
VISAS

NOTICE:
In May, 2011, President Calderon signed into law the new *Ley de Migración* (Immigration Law), which replaces the old system of visas. The old "Tourist visa" (the former *FMM, or Forma Migratorio Multiple*), *Forma Migratorio 2 (FM2), Forma Migratorio 3 (FM3), No-Inmígrate* and *Inmígrate* visas have all been superseded by a new visa credential termed the *Tarjeta de Residencia*. There are four sub-categories of this new visa:

1. *Visitante*. This status covers 6 types of visitors:
A. The non-working tourist
B. The working visitor who has obtained a work permit allowing them to work for an artistic, sporting, cultural, or academic institution under an inter-institutional agreement between a foreign institution and a corresponding Mexican institution
 C. Prospective adoptee parents
D. Visitors on a humanitarian mission
E. *Visitantes Regionales*, or residents of a country which borders Mexico who:
      a. will stay in Mexico less than three days and;
      b. will receive no remuneration in Mexico, and;
      c. will not leave the frontier zone while in Mexico
F. Residents of the US, Guatemala, and Belize who are working in a frontier zone under a frontier-worker program.

None of these visitors may stay in the country longer than 180 days, except those in the Frontier-worker program, who may stay for up to 1 year, and the *Visitante Regional*, who may only stay for three consecutive days, but may leave and re-enter as often as they like. However, any *Visitante* may leave and then re-enter the country after obtaining a new *Visitante* credential at the border once their initial *Visitante* status has expired. There is no limit to the number of times, or how frequently, a person may do this. If you arrive in Mexico by commercial airline or cruise ship, the fee for this visa is included in the price of your ticket. If you arrive on foot, by private boat, private plane, or private automobile, you must pay a fee of around $20USD for the visa. This fee must be paid at a *Banjercito* Mexican bank and most US/Mexico border crossings have a branch located inside, or adjacent to, the Mexican customs/immigration office.

With a *Visitante* visa in hand, the bearer is allowed into Mexico, along with a certain amount and type of personal items (see list below). The bearer may bring his personal vehicle into Mexico, subject to a Temporary Import Permit; see the rules under the section **MOVING YOUR STUFF TO COZUMEL.**

If you plan on staying in Mexico for more than 180 days at a time, opening a Mexican bank account, working and being paid in Mexico, or becoming a Mexican Permanent Resident or Mexican Citizen, you will need to apply for one of the following three other types of visas:

2. Residente Temporal. This status is basically the same as the old *FM3* or *No-Inmigrate* visa, and is an annually-renewable visa that will allow the bearer to reside in Mexico for up to 4 years. It will allow the bearer to work for remuneration in Mexico with the corresponding work permit. You may be denied a renewal for various reasons, but if you live in a manner that is not detrimental to Cozumel's best interests, a denial is unlikely. After 4 years, you have to either leave the country and start proceedings for a new *Residente Temporal* visa or apply for and receive *a Residente Permanente* visa. You may enter and exit Mexico as many times as you want while maintaining the *Residente Temporal* status. The dependent spouse, children, or parents of a *Residente Temporal* also may be admitted into Mexico as *Residentes Temporales.*

3. Residente Temporal Estudiante. This status covers students visiting Mexico to study, train, research, or work on their university degrees.

4. Residente Permanente. This status includes most of the foreigners who previously qualified for the old *FM2* and *Inmigrante* visas. The *Residente Permanente* allows you to live in Mexico indefinitely, similar to a Permanent Resident or "Green Card" holder in the US. This status can be obtained by:

A. Retires living on a pension *(Rentistas)* which provides "sufficient funds to live in Mexico." Previously to this new law, the rules for establishing the amount of funds necessary to live in Mexico under the old *FM2* visa were spelled out as 400 times the basic Mexican minimum wage in Mexico City. Each dependent increases the amount needed by 50%.

B. *Residentes Temporales* who have lived in Mexico for 4 years

C. Those applicants who qualify by the point system. These points are granted based on an applicant's skills, education, and aptitude at activities necessary to Mexico's growth.

D. The spouse and children of the *Residente Permanente.*

E. Asylum seekers and refugees.

F. Parents of children born in Mexico.

G. The children or grandchildren of a Mexican citizen who obtained their Mexican citizenship by birth.

H. A foreign spouse or concubine of a Mexican citizen after two years of living together while the applicant spouse or concubine had a valid *Residente Temporal* status.

The application process

Application for *Residente Temporal* status must within 30 days of entering Mexico if you entered with a *Visitante Visa*. It can also be applied for outside of Mexico at a Mexican Consulate, unless the applicant is applying because he has been offered a job by a Mexican company, he has immediate family living in Mexico, or for any humanitarian reason, in which case the application may be made at the local *oficina de migracion* in Cozumel.

If you are applying at a Mexican Consulate, the Consulate will affix a special form to your passport after you fill out the application and pay the application fee. Once the form is attached, you have 365 days to make your move to Mexico. Once here, you need to go to the immigration office (the *Instituto Mexicano de Migración,* or *IMM*) within 30 days to complete the process. Their office in Cozumel is on the corner of Av. 15 and Calle 5. If you are qualified to start the application process *after* you have already arrived in Mexico, you will first need to go to the website **www.inami.gob.mx/index.php/page/Solicitud de Estancia,** and fill out the online application form. After filling out the online form and receiving your application ID number (called a *Pieza*), you will then go the immigration office to fill out the *Formato Básico* and give them 5 color photos of a small size called *infantile*, including 3 frontal views and 2 right profiles. No jewelry may appear in the photos. Along with the 5 photos, your *Visitante* visa, proof of Mexican residency (a Mexican utility bill in your name or a letter from your landlord), proof of income if you are applying as a *Rentista* (usually your last three monthly bank statements), your marriage certificate if you are married and the birth certificates of any of your children you bring with you. If you are a US citizen, these certificates must have an *apostile* (a certification required by the Hague Convention of 1961) from your home state in the US; see **www.hcch.net** on how to get an *apostile*. If you are a Canadian citizen, these certificates must be certified by a Mexican Consulate in Canada. You must fill out a separate *Formato Básico* for each dependent. After all this is done, the immigration office will give you a password to access your file and a form to take to the bank so you can pay the processing fee there. After you pay the fee, the immigration office will issue you the *Residente Temporal* visa, which looks like a small, plastic ID card. With this visa, you can open a Mexican bank account, sign up for utility services, etc. If you wish to leave Mexico for any reason while waiting for your visa to be granted or renewed, you must apply for a *Permiso de Salida y Regreso* at the immigration office. There are no restrictions on how many times a *Residente Temporal* visa holder may leave and re-enter Mexico, nor are there limits on how long they can be outside of Mexico

The *Residente Permanente* allows you to live in Mexico indefinitely, similar to the Permanent Resident or "Green Card" holder in the US. The process for obtaining a *Residente Permanente* is the same as that for obtaining a *Residente Temporal* visa, only the requirements are different. You may not have a foreign-plated car in Mexico if you hold a *Residente Permanente* visa with a working permit, but <u>are</u> allowed to keep one if you qualified for your *Residente Permanente* visa as a *Rentista*.

Chapter 11
WORK PERMITS

The Ministry of the Interior (*Secretaría de Gobernacíon*) will grant work permits to people with specific skills required in Mexico and to people sponsored by either Mexican companies or foreign companies that operate or have subsidiaries in Mexico. You can also enter Mexico under a *Visitante* visa to work for a foreign company provided that you do not receive any remuneration directly from a Mexican company or subsidiary.

If you want a work permit to work for a Mexican company or a foreign company that operates or has a subsidiary in Mexico you need to gather together the following list of documents:

• Your valid passport and copies of each page of it and its covers

• Your original birth certificate (or official copy, issued from the County Registrar's Office of the county you were born) with a stamp of authenticity issued by the Mexican Consulate nearest your place of birth if you are Canadian, or a apostille issued by the Secretary of State of your birth state if you are American.

• A letter offering you (with your full name) a job from the company for which you wish to work, stating the date they want you to start, the position you will hold, your salary, and typed on the company's letterhead. The letter must be signed by an official of the company whose name appears in the company's *Acta Constitutiva*, the document issued by the Mexican government that establishes the company.

• A copy of identification of the official who signed the offer letter

• A notarized copy of the company's *Acta Constitutiva*

• A copy of the company's most recent quarterly tax declaration *(Ultima Declaración de Impuestos de la Institución)*

• Four color, non-polaroid photographs of the frontal view and four profile shots, with your hair off of your forehead and your ears showing

Once you have gathered your documents, take them to the local immigration office (located on Av. 15 and Calle 5) 30 days before you are scheduled to begin work and start the process for your visa and work permit.

Chapter 12
OTHER DOCUMENTS

Passports

Be sure to register your passport at the appropriate consulate. That way, if it is lost or stolen, it is much easier to replace.

Consular Agency of Canada

Plaza Paraíso Caribe, Modulo C, Planta 2, Oficina C21 - 24
Av. 10 Sur entre Calle 3 y 5 Sur, M-35, Lote 1
Colonia Centro 77710 Playa del Carmen, Quintana Roo - Mexico
Telephone: (984) 803-2411
Fax: (984) 803-2665
E-mail: crmen@international.gc.ca
Hours of Operation Monday - Friday: 9:00 am - 1:00 pm

Mexican Driver's License

To get your Mexican Driver's License, go to the *Direción de Trafico*, which is the building between the *Ayuntamiento* (City Hall) and the parking lot in front of Chedraui between the hours of 8 AM and 1:30 PM, M-F. As you enter the front door, take the hallway immediately to the left and go down it to the door marked *"Licencias."* Take with you the following items:

• Your original passport and a copy of the page with your photo

• Original and copy of your *FM2, 3* or *Carta de Residencia*

• Original and copy of the front and back of your Canadian or US driver's license

• Your *CURP* (it should be on your *FM2, 3* or *Carta de Residencia)*

• The results of a blood-type test from a clinic, showing your type

• A recent copy of your light, water, or land-line phone bill

• 2 color *"infantile"* size photos, frontal view

• A letter-size manila file folder

• 438 pesos for auto license, 511 pesos for *chofer* (chauffeur) (a commercial chauffeur license is required if you drive a pick-up or some types of vans.)

Even if you have a valid foreign license, you must take a written test in Spanish, and a behind-the-wheel test. If you do not speak Spanish, you will need to provide your own translator.

After the tests, they will take your photo and ask for your address, telephone number of your place of business (if any), and home phone. A digital image of your fingerprint and signature will be captured and a plasticized license will be produced while you wait. Your Mexican driver's license will be valid for the same length of time as you are given in your immigration document. You will be allowed to retain your US or Canadian driver's license.

CURP number *(Clave Unica de Registro de Población)*

The *CURP* is the official Mexican ID number, like the US Social Security number. It will be assigned to you the first time you are issued a *Residente Temporal* or *Residente Permanente* visa, and it will appear on the front of your *Residente* card. The *CURP* number is composed of 18 characters arranged as follows:

The first surname's initial and first inside vowel; the second surname's initial (or the letter "X" if, like some foreign nationals, the person has no second surname); the first given name's initial; date of birth (2 digits for year, 2 digits for month, and 2 digits for day); a one-letter gender indicator (H for male, or M for female); a two-letter code for the state where the person was born; for persons born abroad, the code NE (nacido en el extranjero) is used; the first surname's first inside consonant; The second surname's first inside consonant (or the letter "X" if, like some foreign nationals, the person has no second surname); the first given name's first inside consonant; and two characters ranging from 1-9 for people born before 2000 or from A-Z for people born since 2000. For married women, only maiden names are used.

RFC number *(Registro Federal de Contribuyente)*

To obtain a *RFC* number you must apply at the *Secretaria de Hacienda y Crédito Publico,* the equivalent of the U.S. IRS. You must have a *RFC* number to report and pay Mexican taxes for your business or to pay any personal taxes in Mexico.

Apostilles

For many applications in Mexico, you will need the original document (birth certificate, marriage license, etc.) apostilled. The apostille is a certificate required by the Hague Convention of 1961 that confirms the authenticity of the notary public's signature on the original document. If you are a US citizen, the apostille must be issued by the state in which the original document was issued; To see how to get an document apostilled, see **www.hcch.net/en/instruments/specialised-sections/apostille**. If you are a Canadian citizen, original documents must be certified by a Mexican Consulate in Canada, since Canada is not a signatory to the convention.

NOTE: The following chapter is an interpretation of the Mexican rules and regulations regarding the importation of goods into Mexico. Each customs inspector is an individual, and as such, he or she may interpret the rules slightly differently.

Chapter 13
MOVING YOUR STUFF TO COZUMEL

Items Allowed into Mexico with a *Visitante* visa

New or used personal items, such as clothing and toiletries, are allowed so long as they are in accordance with the duration of the trip, and their quantity does not suggest that they can be commercialized. (Note: you can only bring clothing that belongs to you personally; you cannot bring in clothing for someone not accompanying you on the trip.) Besides the personal items, each *Visitante* visa holder is also allowed:

• Two cameras or video cameras, and one video recorder and their power sources; 12 rolls of unused film or video cassettes; photographic material;

• Two cellular telephones; one laptop computer or notebook; a copier or portable printer; a portable projector, and accessories

• Two sports items, four fishing rods, three surfboards (with or without sails) and their accessories, trophies, one stair climber, and one exercise bicycle

• One portable radio/tape recorder; or a digital music player; or a portable compact disc player/recorder and a DVD player/recorder, and a pair of portable speakers and their accessories

• Five laser discs, 10 DVD discs, 30 compact discs, 10 audio cassettes and 5 storage devices or memory cards for any electronic equipment.

• Books and magazines, in quantities not suggesting that they could be the object of commercialization

• Five toys, including collectibles, baby travel items, including hygiene and toys, car seat, crib, walker, and accessories,

• One video game console with video games

• One blood pressure measurement device; one glucose measurement device; medications for personal use in reasonable amounts (in the case of psychotropic or Schedule 2 or 3 drugs, the medical prescription should be present)

• One pair of binoculars and one telescope

• Valises, trunks and suitcases as necessary

• Passengers 18 years old, or older, may bring in up to 20 packs of cigarettes, 25 cigars or 200 grams of tobacco and up to three liters of alcoholic beverages and six liters of wine

• Baby accessories, such as strollers and baby-walkers

• Two musical instruments and their accessories

• One camp tent, camping equipment, and accessories

• Handicapped or older travelers may bring assistance items for personal use, such as walkers, canes, wheelchairs, and crutches

• A set of tools including its case, 1 drill,

• Bedding, including a set of sheets and pillowcases, a set of towels, a set of bath towels, a set of table linen, and a set of kitchen implements

• Two dogs or cats and their accessories, (pet food and used pet bedding may be disallowed) provided that they have their zoo-sanitary import certificates.

You can also bring gifts with a value of up to $50 dollars per person, or $250 dollars per family of five.

You are also allowed in addition to the above items, merchandize valued at $300 dollars or less (with its invoice) if arriving by air; $75 dollars if arriving by ground transportation (unless during Holy week, summer, New Year, or Christmas, when the land allowance is the same as the air allowance). For the specific dates of these periods, see the web site **www.sat.gob.mx/aduanas/pasajeros/Paginas/Mercancia_ingresar_Mexico.aspx**

If you bring a desktop computer, you must pay duties (.008 percent) and taxes (16% at border, 11% at airport), as long as the value of the computer and its peripherals and accessories do not exceed US$4,000. If the total value of the computer and its peripherals and accessories exceeds US$4,000 you must hire the services of a customs broker.

If the total value of duty-free items exceeds $3,000 dollars (not including the desktop computer), you may be required to hire a customs broker to handle your paperwork. If the total of duty-free goods is under $3,000 dollars, you may enter the goods without a customs broker and pay only the IVA of 16% if by ground transportation, or 11% if arriving at a Quintana Roo airport as your first entry-point into Mexico. Payment may be made in advance through the internet at **www.banjercito.com.mx** under "Payment of Foreign Trade Duties"

Once your duty is paid, you must press a button on the stop light. If you receive a green light, you may be on your way. If you receive a red light, the officials will inspect your merchandise to make sure you paid the correct duty.

Failure to declare items may result in a fine of 115% of the total amount of the value of the items undeclared. If entering by private vehicle, the vehicle carrying the undeclared goods may also be forfeited.

Prohibited Items

If any of the following prohibited items are found, they will be confiscated. If guns, ammunition, or illegal drugs are found, you will go to jail. Firearms and ammunition are strictly forbidden, except specially permitted sporting guns for hunting purposes. Sporting guns must meet the requirements outlined in section 4 of the Manual of Tourist Entry. Permission to import sporting guns must be applied for at a Mexican Consulate inside the US or Canada before you enter Mexico.

Other prohibited items include:

Fresh or frozen meat, cheese, eggs, milk, yogurt

Plants and plant material

Fruit, vegetables, seeds and spices

Gasoline other than what is in your vehicle's gas tank

Live predator fish

Turtles, turtle eggs, or products made from turtle

Poppy seeds or poppy-seed flour

Marijuana (*Cannabis indica*), marijuana seeds, medication prepared with marijuana, or extracts, mucilage, or condensed products of marijuana

Juice and extracts of opium, prepared to smoke

Heroin, as a base or hydrochloride of diacetylmorphine

Medication prepared with acetyl morphine or its salts or its derivatives

Thallium sulfate

Isodrin, Aldrin, Heptachlor, Drinox, Endrin, Mendrin, Nendrin, Hexadrin, or Leptophos insecticides

Goods declared "archaeological monuments" by the *SEP* (the Secretariat of Public Education

What a *Residente Temporal* or *Residente Permanente* visa holder may bring into Mexico

To bring your household items in with you into Mexico on a one-time-only basis and within 90 days of receiving the visa, you must first complete a *menaje de casa*, a manifest listing all the items, brands, models, serial numbers, and their values for customs. This *menaje* must be submitted and approved by a Mexican Consulate in the US or Canada <u>before</u> you enter Mexico. Together with 4 copies of the *menaje*, you will also need to submit to the Consulate 4 copies of your valid passport, 4 copies of your *Residente Temporal* or *Residente Permanente* visa, proof of residence in the country of origin (driver's license will work), and the name of the place where you will be residing in Mexico. A fee will be charged for processing the *menaje.*

Article 90 of the Mexican Customs Law, states all items must be <u>used</u>) not new (personal items, household furniture and personal possessions, such as clothes, books, furniture, appliances, computers, entertainment electronics, musical instruments, and artwork. The artwork must not constitute complete collections for the installation of expositions or an art gallery. You may also bring in scientific instruments and tools necessary for your profession or hobby, but they cannot be of a quantity needed for the installation of laboratories, clinics, or workshops. All items listed as allowed for *Visitante* visa holders are also allowed to be brought into Mexico by both *Residente Temporal* or *Residente Permanente* visa holders.

The list of prohibited items is the same as the one for the *Visitante* visa holders.

Bringing your pet to Mexico

Pets entering Mexico with their owners (by air, sea, or land) must have a Health Certificate *(Certificado Zoosanitaria de Exportación)* issued by an official authority or by a licensed veterinarian of their home country. This document must be on a vet's letterhead, include his permit number, and dated no earlier than 10 days prior to your arrival in Mexico. It must contain your name, a description of the pet (sex, race, color, etc.), and your final destination in Mexico. It must also state that your pet was examined and found to be in good health, that it has been treated for internal and external parasites within the last 6 months, and it is now free of external parasites. You must also show proof of vaccines against rabies and distemper, administered at the most 15 days before entering into Mexico and that your dog or cat is taking oral anti-flea medication. At the border, take your pet to the zoosanitary kiosk at the port of entry and present the documentation to facilitate your pet's entry into Mexico. There is no entry charge for up to two pets. More than two incur entry fees. The pet's used bedding or similar items are not allowed into Mexico; only one day's worth of pet food is allowed to enter with each pet. If the Mexican veterinary inspector is temporarily unavailable at the time you wish to enter with your pet, the cost of putting the pet up until he is able to inspect it is at your expense. The above regulations refer only to cats and dogs. Other species have different entry requirements, which you can get from the offices of *SAGARPA*, Av. Cuauhtémoc No. 1230, Col. Santa Cruz Atoyac, Del. Benito Juárez, C. P. 03310, México, DF, or emailing **contacto@senasica.gob.mx**

Importing your vehicle into Mexico

A foreign registered vehicle can be temporarily imported for a maximum period of 180 days. The permit issued will be valid for multiple border crossings. A Temporary Import Permit may be had by applying at one of the *designated* Mexican Consulates (not all offer this service), over the internet with *Banjercito*, or at some *designated* (not all offer this service) US/Mexican border crossings.

You can get a jump on things by getting your Temporary Import Permit while you are still in the US or Canada by accessing the *Banjercito* website, **www.banjercito.gob.mx,** and fill in the application via the internet. Follow the directions and you will receive a permit and your holographic sticker in the mail.

Vehicle liability insurance is compulsory for foreign-plated cars entering Mexico. Good policies may be purchased in the US or Canada through American Automobile Association (AAA) or the Canadian Automobile Association (CAA). See the section on **PRIVATE TRANSPORTATION** for a list of more automobile insurance companies.

Applying for the Temporary Vehicle Import Permit at the border

At the Mexican port of entry (make sure the one you chose is one authorized to issue permits), you must present your valid passport, your Mexican visa, the vehicle's original certificate of registration, the original vehicle title or a document that certifies legal ownership of the vehicle (original and photocopy. If there is a lien on the vehicle, a notarized letter from the lienholder authorizing you to take the vehicle into Mexico), your valid driver's license (original and photocopy), $51.04 USD for the permit fee (the fees change every six months according to law), an international credit card issued outside of Mexico (American Express, Diner's Club, VISA or Master Card) in the name of the owner of the vehicle. You must leave a deposit (cash or credit card charge) of from $200 USD to $400 USD (depending on the age of the vehicle) which they will keep as surety.

After inspecting and accepting your documents, the customs official will inspect your vehicle, photograph the Vehicle Identification Number (VIN) plate, affix a holographic sticker to the inside of your windshield, and give you a customs declaration detailing the temporary import of your vehicle. This form must be returned at the border crossing if you leave Mexico again with your vehicle. At that time, your credit card will be refunded the amount of the surety, or your cash deposit refunded, and you will be given a receipt. If the declaration form is not returned, the bond or surety deposit will be forfeited and you will not be allowed to import another vehicle into Mexico.

How long can you keep the car in Mexico?

Article 106 of the Mexican Importation Law says that your car registration is valid in Mexico so long as your visa is valid, regardless of whether or not your foreign plates are expired. This means that if you have a *Residente Temporal* or *Residente Permanente* visa and keep it renewed each year, you can keep your foreign-plated car in Mexico and never have to register it again. However, if you leave Mexico with your car after the initial 180 days, you must turn in the permit and sticker at the border when you leave and buy a new permit when you return. See the section on **PERSONAL TRANSPORTATION** for more details.

Authorized drivers

Section IV of the article says the vehicle can be driven in Mexico by the owner/importer, his or her spouse, their parents and grandparents, their decedents, their brothers or sisters, or by a foreigner who has the same immigration category as one of those herein referenced, or by a Mexican citizen, provided in this latter case, that a person authorized to drive the vehicle is within the vehicle. Once inside Mexico, you must keep the holographic sticker on the windshield and a copy of the registration paper in the vehicle. A copy of your current visa and passport should always be with you as well. See the section on **PERSONAL TRANSPORTATION** for more details.

Chapter 14
PETS & WILD ANIMALS

Keeping wild animals as pets

In Mexico, many wild animals are protected under Mexican Federal Law as well as the international convention known as CITES. What this means, is that it is illegal to own or keep many types of wild animals, including all types of iguanas, monkeys, parrots, toucans, song-birds, coatis, armadillos, and boas without a special permit. These permits are only issued by *SEMARNAT*, whose nearest offices are in Chetumal and Cancun. You can go to their web page **www.gob.mx/semarnat** for more information. The fine for keeping one of these prohibited animals ranges from a minimum of 40,000 pesos to a maximum of 200,000 pesos. In Cozumel, the laws regarding wild animals and the environment are enforced by the folks at *Media Ambiente y Ecología*. Their office is located near the cenote park on Av. 8 de Octubre.

Injured wild animals

If you encounter an injured wild animal and wish to rescue it, remember these Federal laws prohibiting the keeping of wild animals cover even well-intentioned good Samaritans. You can either call animal control (number below) or take it directly to *Media Ambiente y Ecología* and they will nurse it back to health and then release it. If you would like to volunteer as a "temporary mother" for some of these injured animals, you can apply at *Media Ambiente y Ecología*, and they will call you when they have an animal in need of temporary care and feeding.

Animal control

If you are having trouble with wild animals getting into your garbage, digging in your garden, or annoying your pets. The Cozumel Humane Society will loan you a live trap, if you leave a deposit.

Endangered species found on the island

Cozumel has several endangered animal species and some of them are only found here on the island and nowhere else. They are: Cozumel Harvest Mouse, Cozumel Island Coati, Agouti, Cozumel Pygmy Raccoon, Cozumel Pygmy Fox, Cozumel Thrasher, Cozumel Vireo, Cozumel Wren, Great Curassow, Cozumel Emerald Hummingbird, Crocodile, Toucan, Yucatan parrot, Jabiru, Iguana, Key deer, White-lipped Peccary, and Spider monkey. For a list of endangered sea-life, see the section on **WATER SPORTS**. Several plant species found on the island are also protected, like the Chit Palm and mangrove.

Cozumel Humane Society offers free spay/neutering, live traps, and pet adoptions. **www.humanecozumel.org** cell 044-987-112-3376

CIEMA (*Centro para la Conservación, Investigación, y Educación del Medio Ambiente*) is a non-profit wild animal rescue and rehabilitation program. At Oasis Animal Hospital, Av. 25 between Calles 11 and 13 Sur, **info@ciemainternational.org**

Chapter 15
BANKING

Currency and coins

US currency circulates freely in Cozumel, but nobody will accept a bill that is torn. Large transactions of US cash (like buying a house) are prohibited by law. US or Canadian coins will not be accepted by anyone and cannot be exchanged for pesos at any bank or currency exchange.

Mexican peso bills come in 20, 50, 100, 200, 500, and 1000 pesos denominations. The 1000 peso note should be avoided, as it has been widely counterfeited. The 500 peso notes can also present a problem in change-making at smaller shops and restaurants. Common coin denominations are 1, 2, 5, and 10 Pesos. There are also 5, 10, 20, and 50 *centavo* (cents) coins, but you'll rarely see these, except in change from large chain stores. In addition, there are 20 and 100 peso coins that are in circulation, but not found as frequently as the rest of Mexico's coinage.

Traveler's checks

Most currency exchange houses will change traveler's checks and will give you the same rate as if they were cash. However, some of the 'off-brand' traveler checks may not be accepted; best to use the American Express or VISA brand. Banks usually has long lines here on the island are not really interested in changing travelers checks, but some will.

ATMs

The easiest way to change money in Cozumel is to use your ATM card. You get the best exchange rate and there are no lines. The drawbacks are most US banks will charge you around 2% as a transaction fee (more for cash advances on credit cards), a foreign exchange charge of up to 3%, and most ATMs here will only give you a maximum of 3000 pesos per transaction.

Checks drawn on US banks

US Checks cannot be cashed at banks in Cozumel, but can be deposited into a checking or interest-bearing account. Bear in mind, however, it will take over a month to clear, and a hefty fee will be charged for the service.

Opening a bank account in Mexico

This will take much longer than you are accustomed. First, you must be a Mexican citizen or have a *Residente Temporal* or *Residente Permanente* visa to open an account. A tourist visa or *Visitante* visa will not suffice. Next, you need to bring to the bank:

1. Your passport and a copy (first page only)

2. Your visa and a copy (front and back)

3. A recent copy of your light, phone, or water bill, or a copy of the lease to your home here on Cozumel

Cash Transactions

In an effort to combat money laundering, the Mexican government has recently implemented new restrictions on cash transactions involving US dollars. The maximum amount of US dollars that can change hands in one transaction is $250. This limit does not apply to cash transactions involving Mexican pesos.

Currency Exchanges (*Casas de Cambio*)

Casas de Cambio are located throughout the city, and come and go as the economy dictates. Most do not require any ID for changing currency, but will ask for it to change travelers' checks. Their rates of exchange are usually posted outside their doors.

Banks

Banamex/Citibank Av. Coldwell between Calle 1 & Salas (987) 872-3411

Bancomer Av. 5 between Juárez and Calle 1 *(parque)*, 872- 0550

Bancomer Av. Coldwell between Calle 12 & Calle 10, 872-7010

Banamex Av. P.J.Coldwell at 1ra sur, 987-272-3411

Banorte ATM Av. Quintana Roo between Av 25. and Av. Coldwell

Banorte Av. 5 between Juárez and Calle 2, (987) 872-0718

HSBC, Av. Pedro Joaquin Coldwell at Av. Q. Roo, (987) 872-3080

HSBC Av. 5 at Calle 1, (987) 872-0142, 872-0182

Santander Av. 15 between Calle 3 and Morelos (987) 872-2853

Scotia Bank, Av. 5 at Calle 2, 987-872-9001, 872-4876

Bank Hours

Most banks are open 9 AM to 4 PM, Monday through Friday. A few are open Saturday. See the **CALENDAR** section for bank holidays

Account types

Personal accounts *(persona fisica)* can only have bank account in Mexican pesos. Business accounts *(persona moral)* can have accounts in either US dollars or Mexican pesos.

Interest-bearing accounts

If you have a bank account in Mexico that pays you interest, the bank will withhold a small percentage (0.5%) back for Mexican income taxes. If you are not a Mexican Tax Resident, this is all you will have to pay on this interest income and you do not need to file a Mexican tax return. If you are a Mexican Tax Resident, you can credit this amount on your annual

Mexican tax return. (See "interest bearing accounts" the section on **TAXES**). Soon, however, the US FATCA act may require the Mexican banks to withhold 30% of that interest for the US IRS if you are a "US person" (See "FATCA" under the section on **TAXES**).

Money transfers

Transferring money from your account outside of Mexico to your account inside of Mexico (or vise-versa) can be accomplished in a couple of ways. You can make a wire transfer directly from your foreign bank into your account in a Mexican bank for a small transfer fee and the rate of exchange will be the prevailing bank rate. You can also set up an account with Western Union Online FX and have them make the transfer online.

Western Union

Inside Elektra at Av. Q. Roo between Av. 5 and 10

Av. Pedro Joaquin Coldwell between Salas and Calle 1

At the Telegraph office, next door to the Post Office at Calle 7 and Av. Rafael Melgar.

Xoom

This service that lets you send and receive cash through your bank or credit card by using your cell phone is located in Electra on Avenida Andrés Quintana Roo, just past the park that is in front of the city hall.

Credit cards

Most hotels, large stores, and larger restaurants accept MasterCard and Visa, but most small "Mom and Pop" shops do not take plastic. Discover cards and American Express cards are accepted by very few locations other than large hotels. Most US cards charge a 2% to 3% "foreign transaction fee" on each charge. CapitalOne is one company that does not charge this fee.

Money laundering laws

Mexican citizens can make deposits or payments of up to $4,000 USD in cash or 15,000 pesos cash per month through their bank, but foreigners or Mexicans who don't have bank accounts are limited to $1,500 USD per month. US cash deposits and payments by businesses dealing with tourists and foreigners in Cozumel and other tourist areas will be limited to 14,000 USD a month. Electronic or non-cash (checks or travelers checks) transactions will not be affected.

Bringing cash into Mexico

You can cross the border into Mexico with more than $10,000 USD cash but you have to declare it. Amounts of cash less than $10,000 USD are not required to be reported when entering Mexico. Failure to declare can cost 20-40% of the amount undeclared in fines, plus jail time.

IDE tax on bank deposits

There is a 3% tax on cash deposits over $15,000 pesos per month to any bank account. Deposits made in US dollars are not taxed, but are limited to certain amounts (see above).

FATCA (Foreign Account Tax Compliance Act)

The US recently (March 2010) implemented a new and far-reaching law that includes a new interpretation of what "US persons" will need to report to the US IRS, in addition to the FBAR report. The first part of the law determines who a "US person" is: US citizens, US green card holders, and certain non-US citizens who have stayed in the US for over 183 days during each of the past three years. Country of residence or tax residence does not come into play. The second part of the new law addresses what will be taxed. All foreign assets, income, interest, trusts, *Fideicomisos*, shares in entities (like Limited Liability Companies, Corporations, and partnerships) stocks, security, bank accounts, and accounts in stock trading houses that are owned by a "US person" that total in aggregate over $50,000 USD during any one day of that tax year must now be reported to the IRS by all foreign banks and financial institutions, or else the US will "withhold" a substantial amount of that financial institution's funds that pass through the US. However, just because your total foreign assets sum up to less than $50,000 may not preclude a financial institution from reporting them anyway under this new system. A "US person's" penalty for not reporting their income, interest, or interest in such trusts, *Fideicomisos,* accounts or companies themselves on IRS Form 1040 or on IRS Form 8275, 5471, 8858, and/or 8865 is $10,000 to $50,000. Understatement of the amount of tax owed is 20% if not attributable to fraud, 75% if it is. The "look back period" and statute of limitations for audits has been expanded to the previous six years. Penalties for not reporting your interest in a Trust or *Fideicomiso* on IRS Form 3520 and 3520a is 35% of the amount transferred into the Trust or *Fideicomiso*, with the minimum penalty being $10,000 USD. For a more complete description of FATCAs impact on *Fideicomisos,* see "FATCA's impact on *Fidecomisos*, LLC's, partnerships, and corporations owned or partially owned by US Persons" in the section entitled **TAXES**.

Chapter 16
BUSINESS & FINANCES

Mexican business entities

Mexico recognizes two different types of entities for business and tax purposes. The first is a *persona física*, or a real, live individual. As a *persona física*, one may do business as a sole proprietorship and pay taxes on business income at a very low rate, between .5 and 2%, as long as the business meets certain requirements as to size, number of employees, and gross income. The second type of entity recognized is a *persona moral*, which is a partnership. Often a Mexican partnership is referred to by Americans as a "corporation," but corporations do not exist in Mexico, only various kinds of partnerships. One such partnership is a *Sociedad Anónima de Capital Variable (S.A. de C.V.)* which translates to "Anonymous Partnership with Variable Capital." This type of partnership may include *personas físicas* and/or *personas morales*. Another type of partnership is a *Sociedad de Responsibilidad Limitada de Capital Variable (S. de R.L. de C.V.)* or "Partnership of Limited Responsibility with Variable Capital." Americans often equate this type of partnership with an LLC, or "Limited Liability Company." You can also form a Mexican partnership with just a simple contract, which will allow you to avoid the 30% tax bracket that an *S.A. de C.V.* or the *S. de R.L. de C.V.* types of partnerships are taxed.

Forming a Mexican Business Entity

Foreigners <u>are</u> allowed to form and own business entities in Mexico <u>without</u> Mexican partners. You will need the services of a Mexican attorney, a Mexican CPA, and a Mexican *Notario* to navigate the formalities.

Facturas and *notas*

A *factura* is a legal receipt for goods or services. It is the only type of receipt that can be used to deduct business expenses for Mexican businesses. It will include the cost of the goods or services and the *IVA* (*Impuesto de Valor Agregado,* or the valued added tax). A *nota de remission,* or *nota* is an informal receipt you receive from most vendors and is not valid as proof of a tax deductible expense for a Mexican business and will not include *IVA.*

Electronic *facturas* (invoices)

All *facturas* must now be issued electronically rather than on paper.

US dollar Cash transactions over $250

See "cash transactions" in the section on **BANKING.**

Notarios Publicos

A *Notario Publico* is not anything like a Notary Public in the US; he is more like a judge and is appointed by the governor. He is not your advocate, but rather an impartial official that will see that the property and tax laws are followed.

Accountants

The equivalent of a Certified Public Accountant (CPA) in Mexico is a *Contador Público.* They can be further certified in their specialty of *Fiscal* (Tax), *Finanzas* (Finance), *Costos* (Costs), and *Contabilidad y Auditoría Gubernamental* (Accounting and Governmental Audits).

RFC (Registro Federal de Contribuyente)

To obtain a *RFC* number you must apply at the *Secretaria de Hacienda y Crédito Publico,* the equivalent of the US IRS. You must have a *RFC* number to report and pay Mexican taxes for your business or to pay any personal taxes in Mexico.

Chapter 17
TAXES

Living in Mexico, you will be liable for a few Mexican taxes and perhaps even taxes levied by your home country. Mexico is a signatory to several international tax treaties and the one dealing with US citizens stipulates that the country in which you derive over 50% of your income is your *tax residence*. It does not matter where your *legal residence* is. That means if you live in Mexico and get over 50% of your income from Mexico, you will need to pay Mexican income tax. However, the US demands of its citizens that they report all their worldwide income, so you'll still have to file a US income tax report even if you pay Mexican income tax, but you can deduct the amount of Mexican tax paid from the US income taxes you will owe on your US income.

If you need to file US taxes from Mexico, the IRS will only accept mail from DHL Worldwide Express, FedEx International Priority, and UPS Worldwide Express. You can also file online on the IRS website **www.irs.gov.** To pay taxes electronically, log onto **www.eftps.gov** and they will mail you a pin number with which you can pay quarterly or yearly by credit card via computer or phone. For US taxpayers living in Mexico the filing date for income tax is June 15.

Mexican Income Tax or *Impusto Sobre la Renta (ISR)*

Personal *(Persona Fisica)* income earned by Mexican residents in Mexico is taxed at a progressive rate, ranging from 1.92 to 30%. The corporate *(Persona Moral)* tax rate is 30%. Taxable income includes: wages, rental income, capital gains from selling property, interest income, prize winnings, and dividends.

Assets tax *(impuesto al Activo)*

Mexico taxes all business assets at 1.8%

RFC (Registro Federal de Contribuyente)

To obtain a *RFC* number you must apply at the *Secretaria de Hacienda y Crédito Publico,* the equivalent of the U.S. IRS. You must have a *RFC* number to report and pay Mexican taxes for your business or to pay any personal taxes in Mexico.

IMSS

IMSS tax is a Social Security tax levied on wages. If you are employed, usually your employer pays this tax. If you are self-employed or if you hire someone as an employee, then you must pay this tax. See the section **EMPLOYEES.**

Tax on bank deposits in cash (IDE)

Deposits of over 15,000 pesos in cash are taxed at 3%. US dollar deposits are not subject to this tax.

Interest bearing accounts

If you have a bank account in Mexico that pays interest, the bank will withhold a small percentage for income taxes. If you are not a Mexican Tax resident, this is the most you will pay on this income and you do not need to file a Mexican tax return. If you are a Mexican Tax Resident, you can credit this amount on your annual Mexican tax return.

Rental income

Income from rents collected in Mexico by Mexican Tax Residents is taxed at regular income tax rates, after you deduct the actual expenses of running the property or take a flat deduction of 35%, whichever is greater. If you are not a Mexican Tax Resident, you will pay a flat 25% on the gross income. Both Mexican Tax Residents and non-residents may need to charge *IVA*. See the section on **RENTING YOUR HOME OR CONDO**. It has been relatively easy in the past to avoid taxes on Mexican rental income, but some jurisdictions are beginning to crack down on this.

Stock trades

Gains from the sale of securities traded in the Mexico are free of Mexican tax.

Acquisition tax

When buying property the buyer pays a 2% transaction tax on the value of the property.

Predial

The *predial* is the property tax on real estate in Mexico. In Cozumel it is 1% of the value of the property as stated on the *escritura*, or deed.

Tenencia

The *tenencia* is the tax on Mexican-plated automobiles. The tax is based on the value of the car and its age. It is highest the first few years and then it drops down each year until the vehicle is ten years old, after which, it is forgiven. In Quintana Roo, the tax expired in 2012. See the section on **PERSONAL TRANSPORTATION**.

IVA

Another tax you will be paying when you are in Mexico is the *IVA* (*Impuesto de Valor Agregado*, or the value added tax) that is the 16% sales tax added to most everything. Groceries, books and medicine are exempt from *IVA*.

IEPS (Impuesto Especial Sobre Producción y Servicios)

IEPS is a special tax levied on providers and sellers of internet services, cable TV, alcohol, beer, diesel, wagers, energy drinks and cigarettes.

Impuesto Empresarial de Tasa Unica (IETU)

(IEU) is a special 17.5% tax on income derived from the transfer of goods or independent services.

Report of Foreign Bank and Financial Accounts (FBAR)

All US taxpayers who own or can sign on foreign bank accounts that have (or had) over $10,000 USD in them on any one day during the tax year must report those accounts to the IRS on both IRS Form 1040 (due June 15 for ex-pats) and IRS Form TD F 90-22.1 (due June 30). Penalties of up to $10,000 USD can be assessed for non- compliance.

Foreign Account Tax Compliance Act (FATCA)

The US recently (March 2010) implemented a new and far-reaching law that includes a new interpretation of what "US persons" will need to report to the US IRS, in addition to the FBAR report. The first part of the law determines who a "US person" is: US citizens, US green card holders, and certain non-US citizens who have stayed in the US for over 183 days during each of the past three years. Country of residence or tax residence does not come into play. The second part of the new law addresses what will be taxed. All foreign assets, income, interest, trusts, *Fideicomisos*, shares in entities (like Limited Liability Companies, Corporations, and partnerships) stocks, security, bank accounts, and accounts in stock trading houses that are owned by a "US person" must now be reported to the IRS by all foreign banks and financial institutions, or else the US will "withhold" a substantial amount of that financial institution's funds that pass through the US. However, just because your total foreign assets sum up to less than $50,000 may not preclude a financial institution from reporting them anyway under this new system. A "US person's" penalty for not reporting their foreign income, assets, interest, or interest in foreign trusts, *Fideicomisos,* accounts or companies themselves on IRS Form 1040, 8275, 5471, 8858, and/or 8865 is $10,000 to $50,000. Understatement of the amount of tax owed is 20% if not attributable to fraud, 75% if it is. The "look back period" and statute of limitations for audits has been expanded to the previous six years. Penalties for not reporting your interest in a Trust or *Fideicomiso* on IRS Form 3520 or 3520-A is 35% of the amount transferred into the Trust or *Fideicomiso*, with the minimum penalty being $10,000 USD.

FATCA's impact on Mexican *Fidecomisos*, LLC's, partnerships, and corporations owned or partially owned by "US persons"

In late 2010, the US IRS declared Mexican *Contratos de Fideicomiso Translativo de Dominio* to be a type of Foreign Grantor Trust. As of March 18, 2010, Americans that are considered a "US person" by the IRS, and own property worth more than $50,000, via a Foreign Entity (Mexican Corporation, LLC, Partnership, or *Fideicomiso*) are now required to report that information to the IRS annually on IRS Form 1040 plus IRS Foreign Reporting Forms 3520 (due on the date your 1040 is due), 3520-A for Foreign Trusts (due on March 15), 5471 for Foreign Corporations, 8858 for Foreign Disregarded Entities (Single Member Limited Liability Company, similar to an LLC) and 8865 for Foreign Partnerships (these last three due at the same time as your 1040). A penalty of 35% of the amount transferred into the *Fideicomiso* or a minimum of $10,000 USD can be assessed for non-compliance.

Chapter 18
BUYING A HOME
OR CONDO

Fideicomisos

The Mexican constitution created a "Restricted Zone" that includes all land within 100 kilometers of the border, or within 50 kilometers of the coast. This zone includes all of the island of Cozumel. The constitution also stipulates that foreigners may not own land within this Restricted Zone. However, foreigners may be the beneficiaries of a *Contrato de Fideicomiso Translativo de Dominio,* (often shortened to *"Fideicomiso"*) and the bank that contracts the *Fideicomiso* may hold title to residential land in the Restricted Zone for the benefit of the foreigner. Often referred to as a Land Trust and treated by the US IRS as a Foreign Grantor Trust, a *Fideicomiso* is actually a contract between a bank and an individual that was designed specifically to get around the old law disallowing foreigners from owning land in the Restricted Zone.

Mexico's Foreign Investment Law of 1973 (and amended in 1994), stipulates that the *Fideicomiso* is established for a term of 50 years and may be renewed any time during its existence, as many times as necessary, in perpetuity. The bank holds the title to the land for the benefit of the foreigner, but the foreigner can exercise all the rights and privileges of ownership. He may mortgage, sell, pass on to heirs, lease, or rent the property as he sees fit without the need of any approval from the bank. The cost to set up a *Fideicomiso* is around $2,500 USD, and it costs around $600 USD in legal fees per year to maintain it. Non-Residential land within the Restricted Zone may be held by a Mexican partnership and foreigners may be the sole and exclusive stockholders in that entity.

FATCA also increased the reporting requirements of foreign banks on transactions of American to the IRS. For more information see the articles on the Foreign Account Tax Compliance Act (FATCA) and FATCA's impact on Mexican *Fidecomisos*, LLC's, partnerships, and corporations owned or partially owned by US persons in the section entitled **TAXES**.

Buying property

Once you find a property that interests you, a real Estate agent is a near necessity and you will certainly need the services of a Mexican attorney *(abogado)* and a *notario publico*. A *notario publico* is not anything like a notary public in the US; he is more like a judge and is appointed by the governor. He is not your advocate, but rather an impartial official that will see that the property and tax laws are followed. His fees are usually around 2% to 3% of the purchase price of the property.

One of the first things you will need to do before proceeding with a property purchase is verify if the seller holds clear title to the land. Many properties in Mexico are *ejido* land, or land granted in undivided blocks to groups of Mexican nationals by the government, which may not be sub-divided and sold without all the landowners in the group agreeing. This is very difficult to get done. Other properties may not have been properly recorded *(escritura)* in previous sales. Condominiums may not have had their by-laws approved and recorded. A title search is required to weed out these problem properties. Be aware, however, that the "title search" the *Notario Publico* performs is only a verification of the current owner's position and does not delve into past records. A comprehensive title search is only done by a title company when they are issuing a title insurance policy, something you should be sure to get. A copy of the *certificado de libertad de gravamen* will show the owner of record, surface area, classification of property type, the legal description, and whether there are any liens or encumbrances filed against the property. You should also get a certificate of no tax liability *(certificado de no aduedo)*.

Fees associated with residential property closings in Cozumel will run around 4% to 6% of the purchase price. These fees include the *Notario Publico's* fee, the appraisal fee, title insurance, deed recording fee, a transfer tax of 3%, and prorated property tax *(predial)*. Any capital gains tax *(Impuesto Sobre la Renta, or ISR)* due on the sale of the property is the responsibility of the seller. However, if the seller fails to pay the tax, the buyer may be held responsible and required to pay it. Make sure the capital gains tax is placed in escrow or paid in full at the time of the sale.

Your property tax, the *predial*, is currently around 1% of the <u>stated</u> sales price in the *manifestación catastral* (depending on where the property is located). The actual price you paid for the property may be significantly higher than the stated sales price. This custom of understating has been a practice that has come under scrutiny of late and may be disallowed at a future date. There are other reasons not to follow this tradition of understating the value of the purchase. For example, if you understate the price as the buyer, you will save a portion of the 2% transfer tax, as well as a portion of the 1% *predial* tax, but when you go to sell the property, the new buyer may decide to record the actual price he is buying the property for, and you will be billed a 29% Mexican capital gains tax on the difference on what you originally declared as your purchase price, and the real selling price to the new buyer.

Chapter 19
RENOVATION & NEW CONSTRUCTION

Before you begin, talk to others who have built here on the island to get the benefit from their experiences. Ask a lot of questions. Get references of qualified architects, contractors, and tradesmen. Check on costs and availability of construction supplies. Do your homework before working on your home!

Permits

Next, you will need the services of a licensed architect. The architect will submit the plans you have come up with together to the *Desarollo Urbano* (City Planning Commission), and *Media Ambiente*, (Environmental Protection) for approval and building permits.

Contractors

If you decide to hire a contractor to do the work, first you will need to decide whether to get the job bid as "turn-key," or "pay-as-you-go." This second option may work well for people who have the time to be on the job site regularly to keep an eye on things, but if you are not available for stretches of time, this may not be the best way. The "turn-key" option, where the price is based on the square meter, is not the same as what you may understand the term to mean in your home country. It usually only includes the shell of the house (called the *obra negra*) with some of the electricity and plumbing installed but usually does not include painting, light fixtures, plumbing fixtures, windows, doors, counters, tile-work, cabinets, shelving, appliances, etc. Many local contractors try to balance several jobs at once, and if you are off-island for long stretches, your job may be pushed back or delayed to accommodate the others. "The squeaky wheel gets the grease" is the operative phrase in this instance.

Jobsite workers

If you hire a building contractor to remodel or begin a new construction project, he is responsible for the workers he employs. But who will pay the workers' *IMSS* tax must be worked out ahead of time. If the contractor agrees to pay the tax, you must make certain he does so, and on a timely manner, or you will be held responsible, since you are the property owner (or the *Fidecomiso* Beneficiary). Calculating the *IMSS* tax levied against the workers involved in new construction is a little complicated, and based on the amount of tax *IMSS* expects to get from the job based on the total number of square feet. When the job is finished, *IMSS* will calculate how much tax has been paid in, against how much they calculated they would get. If there is a discrepancy in their favor, you will be billed for the difference. This may take as much as a year before the final adjusted bill arrives; long after the contractor has departed. The amount may be substantial.

If you act as your own contractor and hire tradesmen to do work for you on a remodel or new construction project, make sure you hire them by the job, and not by the hour, day, or week. If they are contracted by the job, they are considered independent contractors; as such, they are non-salaried, exempt workers. If you hire them by the hour, day, or week, they are considered your employees, and there is a huge amount of regulations you must become familiar with concerning workers' rights if you don't want trouble. Either way, the voluntary rule still applies; if they want to enroll in *IMSS*, you must enroll them and pay the tax. See the section on **EMPLOYEES** for an explanation of *IMSS* taxes. If the job needs any permits you must register all workers in *IMSS*, regardless of their category.

Chapter 20
EMPLOYEES

If you need to hire a full time or part time employee, be sure to have an accountant go over the labor laws with you. These laws can be quite complex, and as an employer, you carry financial responsibilities that are not the norm in the US or Canada. For example: All employees, except certain exempt ones, must be registered with the *IMSS* and you must pay their *IMSS* taxes. You will need an accountant to set up your account with the *IMSS*, and also set up a *libro de nomina* (record of pay). The workers that are classified as exempt from *IMSS* registration are: artisans, craftsmen, and domestics (maids, cooks, etc.,) who work only in your home. Also exempt are non-salaried workers like those who are paid by the job or by the piece rather than by time worked. These include repair men, handymen, and tradesmen who are contracted to do a specific job on your property that will not take many hours to complete. Home remodeling and new construction is a completely different category, and these workmen need to be enrolled in *IMSS* (see the section on Remodeling/New Construction). By law, exempt workers may elect to be included in the *IMSS* program, in which case you must then enroll them and pay the fees. This is not as bad as it sounds, as it will protect you in case the worker is injured on the job. If an employee is hurt on the job and is not enrolled in *IMSS*, you are responsible for his medical bills as well as continuing full wage while he is off work. If the exempt employee does not want *IMSS* coverage, have him sign an agreement stating that he declines *IMSS* enrollment.

The law requires that all employees, whether exempt or not, be paid weekly in <u>cash</u> the last day worked each week and to be given certain benefits. These benefits include: a Christmas bonus (called the *aguinaldo*), seven paid holidays a year, a paid vacation, paid maternity leave, and a termination pay package. The *aguinaldo* must be paid, in cash, on or before December 20 and it must equal 15 days salary. Vacation pay must be paid in cash before the vacation is taken, or by the end of the year if no vacation was taken. It must equal 6 days salary plus an additional 25% of that amount. The seven paid holidays are the Federal Holidays noted in the Cozumel Calendar section. If a worker works during one of these legal holidays you must pay triple-time. If an employee works on a Sunday, you must pay an extra 25% overtime bonus, no matter how many days a week he works. A female employee is entitled to a maternity leave consisting of the six weeks before a pregnancy and six weeks after, at full pay. If she is unable to come back to work after the initial leave period, she is entitled to 60 more days leave at half-pay.

The termination pay package for employees can be very costly to the employer. If an employee is terminated, (unless for "just cause," which can be very tough to prove in the Mexican legal system and requires a specific process to be followed) he is entitled to three month's salary plus 20 day's pay for each year worked, plus prorated vacation time owed, plus a prorated portion of the upcoming *aguinaldo*. If the termination package is not paid at the time of termination, the terminated employee is entitled to full pay until it is. Even if an employee just stops showing up to work with no explanation, you must be sure to follow up with a report to the labor authority *(Junta de Conciliación y Arbitraje)* to protect yourself from future problems. If you hire more than five employees, they can unionize. If an employee has a problem with you, his pay, his benefits, or his working conditions, he can file a complaint against you with the labor authority and you will need to hire an attorney to represent you at the hearing.

The minimum wage for 2017 in Mexico is 80.04 pesos per day. This minimum wage is not the actual rate workers are paid here, but a figure that is multiplied and used in calculations involving fines, lost wages, and other things. Most workers in Cozumel are paid much more than 80.04 per day For example, a maid may be paid 50 pesos per hour, while a master carpenter may be paid 500 pesos a day.

Chapter 21
UTILITIES

Electrical service

Electrical service on the island is provided by *Comision Federal de Electricidad (CFE)*, whose offices are located at Av. Pedro Joaquín Coldwell between Calles 33 and 35 Sur. They are open Monday through Friday, 7 AM to 4:30 PM. Office phone is (987) 857-2415. They also have automatic teller machines where you can pay your bill at Chedraui at Av. Melgar and Av. Xel-Ha and at Mega on Av. Melgar. You can also pay at any OXXO or 7-11 for a small added service fee.

Voltage on Cozumel is the same as in the US and Canada; 120 volts, 60 Hz. Some of the older buildings may not have grounded outlets that can receive a three-pronged, grounded plug, and you might need an adapter. The *CFE* delivers reliable service, with few surges, but there may be an occasional flicker that will reset some electronic clocks to flashing 12:00. If the power is disconnected by natural causes (heavy rain, hurricane, etc.) the *CFE* is good about getting it turned back on right away. For outages (check first to see if it is only your residence or the whole block) or problems like tree limbs, hung kites, transmission line sparking, humming transformers, loose cables, etc., call their hot-line 071. If that number does not answer, call 987-857-2415. CFE maintains a web page at **www.cfe.gob.mx**

Contracting electrical service

To contract electricity, go to the *CFE* office with your passport and proof of your address (a letter from your landlord, property deed in your name, or a recently paid phone bill showing your address). They will make out a contract and include your deposit in the first billing cycle. *CFE* will come to your home and turn on the power in a couple of days. If you already have electricity running on a previous resident's contract, they will come and read the meter to start billing your account.

Receiving and paying your electric bill

Bills are sent out every two months and come due within 15 days, unless you have a programed electronic meter and a smart card, which is billed monthy and explained farther below. Bills are not mailed out, but instead are usually stuffed under your front door, tucked into a gate hinge, or simply dropped on your door-step, so be aware of the date your bill should arrive and keep an eye out for it. You can also sign up to have it sent to you via email. Accounts that are not paid by the due date have the electrical service cut off right away. If you do not go to the *CFE* office and pay the past-due bill and a re-connection fee within 15 days of the service suspension, your contract will be voided. You can pay in person at the *CFE* office's 24-hour auto-tellers, all banks, *OXXO* stores, 7-Eleven, Sam's Club, YZA pharmacies, Mega, San Francisco de Asis, Soriana, Chedraui, Bodega Aurrera, Coppel and the Telegraph office. These off-site locations can only accept payments up until two days before the due date. After that date has passed, you need to go directly to *CFE* to pay. Not receiving your bill is not considered by *CFE* to be an excuse to not pay it or to pay it late. If you haven't received the bill by the time you know it should have come, take a previously paid bill to the *CFE* office and the bar-code reader on the auto payment machine in the lobby will tell you how much you owe on the bill that never showed up and you can pay it there.

Factors that determine your basic rate per kWh

Electricity is billed by the kilowatt-hour (kWh), but in a VERY complicated manner that takes several things into account in determining your rate. First, there is the region of the country where your meter is located. Cozumel is in *Region Peninsular*. Second, there is the billing sector of your meter. Cozumel is in one of the most expensive sectors, *sector 1C*. Third, electrical service is divided into either commercial or residential; commercial rates are about three times higher than normal residential rates, unless a residence enters the *DAC* rate level, in which case the residential kWh becomes more expensive than the commercial kWh. Fourth, there are two rate seasons, *verano* (April 1 to September 30) and *fuera de verano* (October 1 to March 31). *Fuera de verano* rates are higher than *verano* rates. Fifth, each month has its own rate schedule, adjusted monthly to reflect the cost of energy generation and the national rate of inflation. *CFE* does not post the rates online until after the billing period has expired, so getting an exact handle on pricing for budgeting purposes is next to impossible. Sixth, the kWh rates are based on a subsidy the federal government grants to all residential customers who stay within certain limits of consumption (more about those limits below). However, if you exceed these limits, this subsidy can be taken away, a single punitive kWh rate will be applied to all your electrical usage, and your bill will rise exponentially!

Your kWh billing rate (the following examples are all based on the Oct-Nov 2016 *fuera de verano* residential rates in Cozumel)

The first 25 kWh of a billing period are included in the minimum *(cargo fijo)* and billed at a flat charge of 17.63 pesos.

The next 125 kWh (kWh #26 through kWh #150) are each charged at the *tarifa basica* rate, or .793pesos per kWh.

The next 200 kWh (kWh #151 through kWh #350) of your bimonthly bill are each charged at the *tarifa intermedia* rate, a progressive rate in which each kWh is individually priced, with each succeeding kWh being priced higher than the one preceding it, beginning at .853 pesos for kWh #151 and rising steadily to .956 for kWh #350.

This brings you to the level of usage of 351 kWh per billing cycle. When you hit this level, things take a real turn for the worse! The rate per kWh from 351 kWh of usage and up is the *tarifa excedente* rate, a progressive rate that starts at .993 pesos per kWh and increase steadily to 2.80 pesos per kWh.

DAC (Domestico Alto Consumo)

When you pass 1,700 kWh in a bimonthly billing cycle (850 kWh per month), you move into the pre-*DAC (Domestico Alto Consumo)* category. When you first hit this level of consumption, your kWh cost still continues to be charged at the *excedente* rate, but it is not yet as bad as it can be. However, once you enter this higher level of kWh consumption, the <u>rate you will be charged in the future</u> is in jeopardy of being raised and <u>locked</u>

in at that exorbitant rate until your average usage for the preceding six billing cycles falls below 1,700 kWh! The *CFE* constantly monitors your level of consumption and if your total usage for any preceding 12 month period (or 6 previous billing cycles) climbed to over 10,200 kWh, you lose your government subsidy, your future rate is raised to *DAC* (or a flat rate of 3.755 pesos per kWh), and you are locked in to that high rate as long as your annual consumption is 10,200 kWh or more. Another way to be saddled with the *DAC* rate is to be billed over 10,200 kWh in one billing cycle, in which you go directly to DAC without passing *GO!* The only way to get out of the *DAC* rate lock-in and re-qualify for the subsidy is to either use less than 10,200 kWh total during a 12-month period (6 billing cycles) and hope they notice and then reduce your rate, or cancel your contract and move.

The cherry on top

All these rates carry taxes on top: 16% *IVA* (the value-added tax) and 5% *DAP* (a municipal tax used to pay *CFE* for public street lighting).

Reading your own old-style *CFE* electric meter

If you do not have one of the new digital meters, you will need a little practice reading the old-style 4 or 5 dial meters. Note that each dial turns in the reverse direction of the one next to it. First, mark down the digit that the hand on the far right-hand dial points towards. Use the following two rules:

A. If the hand is between two digits, mark down the smaller of the two. If the hand points between the 9 and 0, write down 0.

B. If the hand is directly over a number, look at the position of the hand on the dial to that dial's right. If the hand on *that* dial has *passed* 0, mark down the number that the hand on the dial you are noting is over. If the hand on the dial to the right has *not* passed 0, note the smaller number next the one the hand is over on the dial you are noting down.

With this 4 or 5 digit number (depending on whether you have a four or five dial meter) in hand, you can go to the *CFE* office and they will give you an estimated reading of how many kWh you have used in this current billing cycle. They also can give you a form with drawings of the dials so you can just mark the positions of the hands and they will figure it out for you.

The new, programed electronic meters

The new electronic meters are programmable, so that they can be used in conjunction with a "smart" card. If you have a new contract made, CFE will require that old mechanical meters be replaced with a programed electronic meter. If you already have an electronic meter when you make a new contract, CFE will require that it be programed. To program the meter, a CFE technician will come to your residence and activate the meter. He will ask you what day of the month you want to pay your bill. It will be a monthly bill, ending on the 1st, 5th, 10th, 15th, 20th, or 25th and then he will enter the day of the month you chose into the meter's memory. He will then give you a smart card, which you must not lose, or you will be charged a replacement fee. You will use this smart card to pay your monthly bill.

The way it works is, when you get to the day of the month you have chosen as the ending date in your monthly cycle, a steady green light will come on in the meter. You then must place your smart card on top of the meter and leave it there for 15 seconds while the meter uploads the usage information into the smart card's chip. You then take your card to the nearest smart card reader kiosk (at the CFE office, Mega, or Chedraui) and pay your bill at the kiosk. The machine will upload the fact that you paid your balance into the smart card's chip. You then must take the card back to your meter and lay it on top of the meter until the green light goes off.

If you fail to pay the bill with your smart card within 10 days after the date you chose as a billing date, the green light will go off and a red light will come on. Once the red light comes on, the meter will shut off and you will be without electricity until you pay the bill and use your smart card to upload the fact that you paid by laying it on top of the meter for 15 seconds.

If all this sounds too complicated and you would prefer to pay bimonthly and have CFE read your meter and send you a bill, you can apply to revert to that old method once you have used the new smart card for three full billing cycles. One reason that you can use to apply for the change is because you "leave the island for extended periods of time and are unable to use the card to read the meter while you are away."

Reading your CFE electric bill

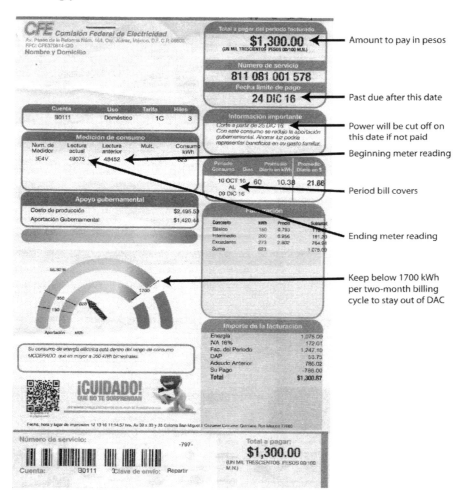

Amount to pay in pesos

Past due after this date

Power will be cut off on this date if not paid

Beginning meter reading

Period bill covers

Ending meter reading

Keep below 1700 kWh per two-month billing cycle to stay out of DAC

Butane gas

The cooking and heating gas available in Cozumel is butane. Butane burns a little cooler than propane (one pound of propane will produce 21,500 BTUs against butane's 21,200) but the difference is negligible.

Most people who don't have a large, stationary tank keep two smaller gas tanks. These smaller tanks come in 10, 20, 30, and 45 kilo sizes. When one tank is empty, you can switch to the full one without interruption. You can take the empty tank to the butane gas filling station or wait until one of the gas trucks comes by your street and let him switch out your empty tank for a full one. The tanks are interchangeable between companies. Both butane gas companies are on Avenida Claudio Canto Anduze, north of Avenida 8 de Octubre.

City water

Although the water distributed by the *Comision de Agua Potable y Alcantarillado (CAPA)* ranks in the top 98 percentile of all Mexican cities based on the quality of their public water supply, there are still problems with it that makes it unsafe to drink. The water comes from deep aquifers under the island and is then chlorinated before it is distributed to the pipes under the city streets. However, since there is occasionally insufficient water pressure to insure contaminated surface water does not infiltrate these underground pipes, and since this lack of pressure also makes it necessary to store city-supplied water in residential cisterns where it can stagnate and become contaminated before it enters the residence's internal pipes, it is best not to use city water for drinking or meal preparation.

Although there are residential water purification systems available (such as reverse osmosis, ozone, and ultraviolet), most people buy bottled water for drinking and food preparation. It is also a good idea to add 20 drops of chlorine (*cloro*) to a gallon of tap water to use to wash and sterilize fruits and vegetables.

CAPA is located on Av. 15 between Av. Benito Juárez and Calle 1 Sur. They provide the city's water and sewer service. Their phone number is 073. You can download the application for water service from their website **www.capa.gob.mx** and take it filled out to their office. If it is a new installation or change of ownership, you will need the title to the property, (or the *orden de ocupación*, the *contrato de compra venta*, or *recibo de pago de tereno)*, your photo ID, a drawing of where the connection will be, and the *cédula catrastral*. If it is only a change of account name for a rental, you will need a copy of the last receipt, a copy of your lease, photo ID, and the *cédula catrastral*. The cost to change ownership is 214 pesos. The cost to open a new contract is 1,2612 pesos plus 16% *IVA*. *CAPA* is open Monday through Friday, 8 AM to 4 PM.

Bills are delivered monthly and stuffed under your door, tucked into your gate, or simply left on the ground if you do not provide a mail box. If you have not received your bill by the time it should have been delivered, you can get a duplicate for around six pesos by applying in person at the *CAPA* office. Bills can be paid at their downtown office, banks, *OXXO* stores, or supermarket checkouts.

Water is charged by the cubic meter. The price changes every month, and if you want to know what it is, you need to go to CAPA's office and fill out and mail in a form requesting the current prices, because the bozo who is in charge of invoicing thinks it is some kind of state secret. In 2016,the minimum charge for 10 cubic meters, was 88.02 pesos. The base charge for usage between 11 and 20 cubic meters was 102.28 pesos, plus 10.82 pesos for each cubic meter after the 11th. The base charge for usage between 21 and 40 cubic meters was 256.68 pesos, plus 16.69 pesos for each cubic meter after the 21st. The base charge for 41 to 60 cubic meters was 612.93 pesos, plus 21.34 pesos for each cubic meter after the 41st. For usage over 60 cubic meters, the basic charge was 1,377.07 plus 52.18 per cubic meter after the 61st. A 5% service fee for chlorination is added to the total. IVA is not charged on the water usage, but is only applied to the sewer portion of the bill; see below.

If you are late in paying your bill, there will be no interest, fine, or penalty added to the amount you owe until it is past 60 days overdue. A penalty of 146.00 pesos will be then added to the amount you owe. If you contact *CAPA* and either pay the bill, or work out a payment schedule within 6 months of getting this penalty, no other penalty fees or interest will be applied. However, if they have not heard from you within this 6-month period, they will cancel your contract, turn off your water, and turn your account over to the *DIRECCIÓN DE RECUPERACIÓN DE ADEUDOS Y EJECUCIÓN FISCAL (DRAEF)*, the state-operated collection agency, who WILL add on interest amounting to around three times what your bill would have been had you paid on time. To reconnect, a special fee of 383.00 plus IVA also will be charged.

CAPA will accept pre-payments on water bills, in the amount you choose to pre-pay, in case you will be out of town for extended periods. Remember, however, if the amount you chose to pre-pay is based on the monthly minimum and your home's water pipes spring a leak somewhere between the meter and your house while you are gone, the bill may be more than the minimum and will be overdue when you return.

If you suspect your home's water supply has a leak somewhere, call CAPA and they will send someone out to check your meter and tell you if you do or not. They will not fix the leak, though, if it is on 'your' side of the meter.

City sewer

CAPA is also responsible for the city sewer system *(systema de drenaje sanitario)* and you must have a water service contract with them before you can have a sewer contract. If you are connecting to the sewer system for the first time, you will need an application to break into the city pipe.

The monthly charge for your sewer connection is also included in your water bill (listed as *drenaje*) and is an additional 35% of your water cost. The minimum amount is 32.60. 16% *IVA* is added to the sewer charge.

Reading your water bill

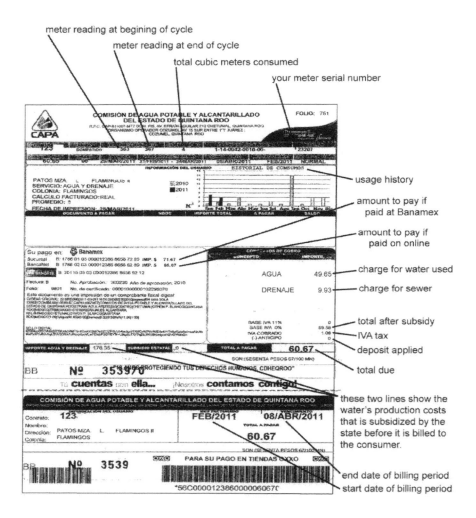

meter reading at begining of cycle

meter reading at end of cycle

total cubic meters consumed

your meter serial number

usage history

amount to pay if paid at Banamex

amount to pay if paid on online

charge for water used

charge for sewer

total after subsidy

IVA tax

deposit applied

total due

these two lines show the water's production costs that is subsidized by the state before it is billed to the consumer.

end date of billing period

start date of billing period

Bottled water

There are several companies in Cozumel that sell purified bottled and all have trucks circulating throughout the town daily. When flagged down, the driver will stop and carry the bottle into your house for you if you ask. Some bottles are interchangeable between companies.

Garbage pick-up & Recycling

The city government provides (through a contract with the private company *PASA*) curb-side residential garbage collection, free of charge. All organic household garbage to be picked up must be in garbage cans or plastic bags. No construction materials, lawn or garden trimmings, recyclables, or large items are allowed on the regular pick-up days, which vary by *colonia* (see map and list below to see the collection days for your area). If you have a large item (like an old stove or refrigerator) call the city at 800-(501) 1234 to schedule a free pick-up. If you have questions regarding your garbage pick-up, call Carina at 869-1900 and she will be glad to help you out. The garbage trucks leave to begin their routes at 10PM on the day they are scheduled to pick-up. The day after *PASA* picks up the garbage, *CAMAR*, the city recycling company, makes the same route to pick up recyclables. These items include: paper, cardboard, glass bottles, cans, PET #1 plastic, HDPE #2 plastic, PP #5 polypropylene, tires, used vegetable oil, and batteries. Batteries must be in a bag and labeled as such. *CAMAR* will make a special trip to pick up large amounts of recyclables if you call 800-501-1234. *PASA* will also make a special trip for extra-large items if requested, or you can take the material yourself to *CAMAR* at Calle 1 between Calle 135 and Calle 140 between the hours of 6 AM and 2 PM Monday through Saturday. Small used batteries also can be disposed at Chedraui, between the cashiers and the entrance nearest the waterfront. It is shaped like a battery.

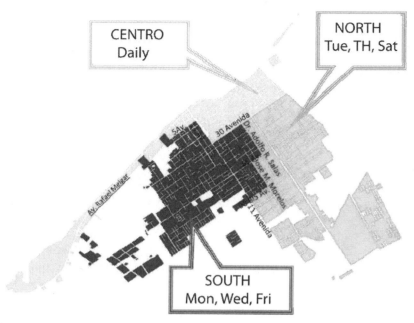

CENTRO
Daily

NORTH
Tue, TH, Sat

SOUTH
Mon, Wed, Fri

Garden trimmings

To dispose of lawn and garden trimmings, take them to the compost heap at *Plantas y Jardines* at kilometer 3.5 on the *carretera transversal.*

Large articles of trash

Seven-ton dump trucks can be hired to pick up large amounts of garbage, waste, or trash and haul it away for around 1200 pesos. The dump truck union's lot at the corner of Av. Presidente Miguel Aleman and Av. 8 de Octubre (where all the dump trucks are parked.) Their phone number is (987) 872-1416. The dump charges an extra 10 pesos per ton to drop the load. The dump truck union also rents out moving trucks. A 3-ton *"camioneta"* with driver costs 800 pesos. You can find day laborers in the parking lot of Mega and the corner of 65th and Juarez in front of Coppel every morning looking for work.

Chapter 22
PUBLIC
TRANSPORTATION

Passenger ferries to mainland

There are three companies providing fast passenger service between Cozumel and Playa del Carmen, two that for around 160 pesos one way for the 30 to 45 minute ride, one that charges for 135 pesos one way. Regular departures leave the municipal pier in front of Las Palmeras Restaurant daily. Typically, the departures are at the top of the hour starting from 5 AM from Cozumel to Playa and 6 AM from Playa to Cozumel, with the last ferry of the day leaving Playa for Cozumel at 11 PM and from Cozumel to Playa at 10 PM, but theses hours are subject to change. For Mexico WaterJet's current schedules, see their website at **www.mexicowaterjets.com** or call them at 872-1508. Call UltraMar 872-3223 or see their website **www.granpuerto.com.mx** for more info. For Barcos Caribe call 897-120-3982, or visit **www.barcoscaribe.com**. Tickets for all three companies can be purchased at the pier. All three companies honor the *Plan Local* discount card and INAPAM senior citizen ID discounts. There is no charge for luggage. Freight (boxes) that can be handled by one or two men will be charged a nominal rate.

Plan Local, the discount plan for locals

Mexico WaterJet and UltraMar passenger ferry companies on Cozumel issue *Plan Local* discount cards that get you a big discount for ferry tickets. Each company honors the other's cards, and Barcos Caribe honors both of them as well. You can apply for this discount card at the *Modulo de Plan* just outside the offices of Mexican WaterJets on Av. 6 Norte between 10th and 15th, or at Ultramar's office at the corner of calle 2 norte and Av. 5. You need the original and a copy of your *Residente Temporal* or *Residente Permanente* visa, proof of residence in Cozumel (current cable, light, or water bill) and 100 pesos. Your picture will be taken and a card issued while you wait. The card is also honored at many local business for discounts ranging from 5 to 30%.

Car/truck ferry to the mainland

TransCaribe runs a vehicle ferry from Calica (also known as Punta Venado) on the mainland (on the Carretera Playa del Carmen-Tulum, Km. 282) to Cozumel and back around six times a day, except Sunday and Monday which have reduced schedules. The voyage takes about one hour and fifteen minutes. For a current schedule and price of tickets, visit the ferry's website **www.transcaribe.net** or call them at 987-872-7688, 987-872-7671, or 987-872-7504. To buy a ticket and board, go to the *API* ferry staging area on Av. Presidente Miguel Aleman, just east of the red light at the car ferry pier south of town before the scheduled departure and you will be given a slip of paper to fill out and sign at the entrance. You will be shown where to line up your vehicle for boarding. Once boarded, take the slip to the cashier on board and pay the fare.

Colectivos

Colectivos are shared vans *(combis)* operated by the taxi union that run along fixed routes with fixed stops. Prices are by the ride, not by the stop or distance. Non-scheduled stops are not allowed. Routes are marked on the van's windshields. All 8 routes begin and end at Chedraui Plaza. They begin running at 6 AM and the last run is at 8 PM, daily, but Sundays the service may be a little delayed, as the supervisors have Sundays off. No animals, smoking, or consumption of alcohol allowed aboard. Cost is 8 pesos adults, 4 pesos children under 3 years or students and seniors with INAPAM ID. Many, but not all, the vans have AC and WiFi. Supervisors are on hand M-Sat at stops at Chedraui, Cl. 35 x Av. 65, and Juarez x Av. 90. There is always an English-speaking supervisor at Chedraui. The main office is in Plaza del Sol, second floor.

Colectivo Route 5 Chentuk-San Gervasio-Repoblador is shown below. It is run by 2 vans, #5-02 and #5-06. One of these two hits each stop every 15 minutes.

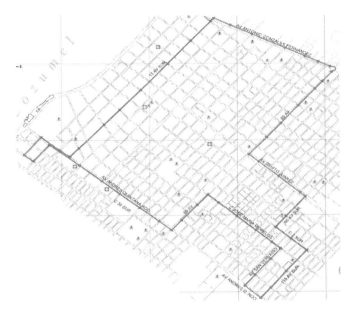

Colectivo Route 8 Emiliano Zapata I, below, is run in a clockwise direction by van #12, which makes each stop every 20 minutes.

Colectivo Route 6 Circuito Colonias Norte (below) is serviced by 2 vans, #6-07 and #6-10. A van passes by each stop every 25 minutes. The route is the same as Colectivo route 6 Circuito Colonias Sur, but in the opposite direction (Route 6 Circuito Colonias Norte travels *clockwise*)

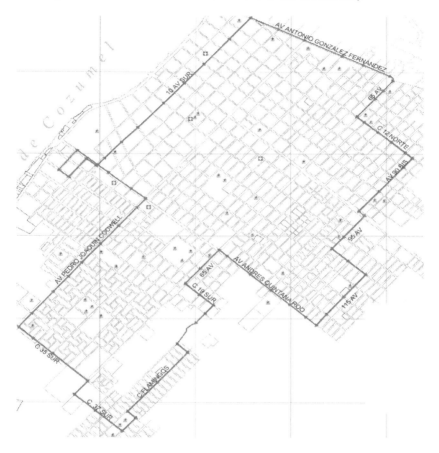

Colectivo Route 6 Circuito Colonias Sur (below) runs the same route as Colectivo Route 6 Colonias Norte, but in the opposite direction (*counter-clockwise*). It is run by vans #6-08 and #6-11 and they pass each stop every 25 minutes.

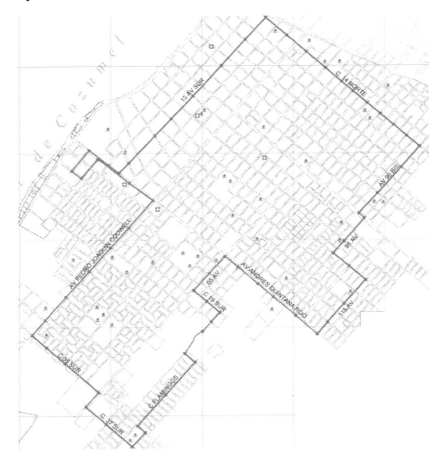

Colectivo Route 9 Ranchito (below) is run by vans #9-03 and #9-18 in a clockwise direction. A van stops by each stop every 20 minutes.

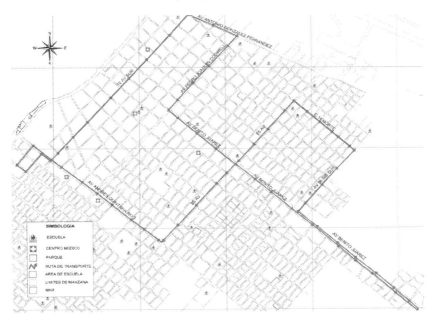

Colectivo Route 1 San Miguel I y II (below) is run by vans #1-01, #1-04, #1-05, and #1-13, traveling in a *counter-clockwise* direction. A van services each stop every 9 minutes.

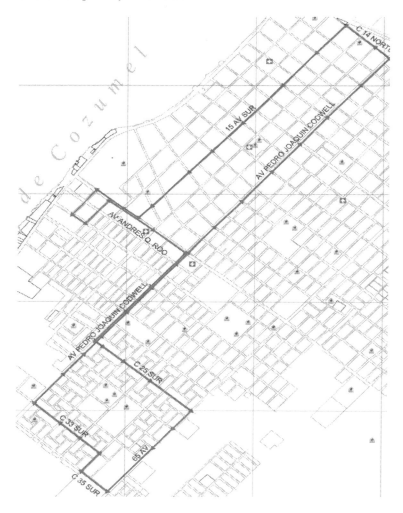

Colectivo Route 7 Circunvalación (below) is serviced by vans #7-09 and #7-14, in a counter-*clockwise* direction. A van comes by each stop every 20 minutes.

110

Colectivo Route 13 Altamar-Miraflores (below) is serviced by vans #16 and #17, in a *clockwise* direction. A van comes by each stop every 20 minutes.

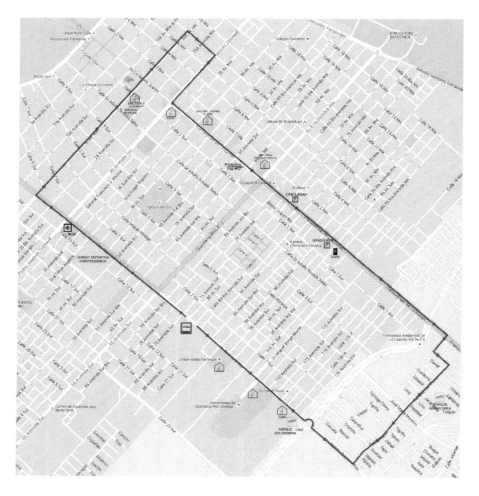

Colectivo Route 14 Zamna (below) is serviced by vans #19, in a *clockwise* direction. A van comes by each stop every 35 minutes.

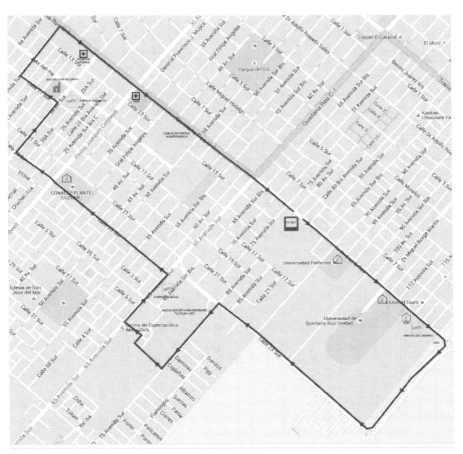

Uniper City Buses

A city bus service runs seven routes around town. Each bus has its scheduled stops written on its windshield. All 8 routes begin and end at Chedraui Plaza. They begin running at 6 AM and the last run is at 9 PM, daily, but Sundays the service may be a little delayed, as the supervisors have Sundays off. No animals, smoking, or consumption of alcohol allowed aboard. Cost is 8 pesos adults, 4 pesos for children under 3 years, or students and seniors with INAPAM ID. Most buses have AC and WiFi. Supervisors are on hand M-Sat at stops at Chedraui, Cl. 35 x Av. 65, and Juarez x Av. 90. There is always an English-speaking supervisor at Chedraui. The main office is in Plaza del Sol, second floor.

Uniper Bus Route Emiliano Zapata I is shown below. It is serviced by Uniper bus #T23, and is run in a clockwise direction. The bus comes by each stop on this route every 30 minutes.

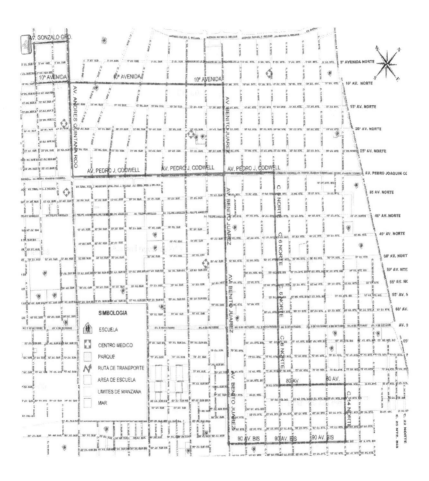

Uniper bus route 7 Circunvalación Norte (below) is serviced by two
Uniper buses, #U14 and #U27, each running in a *clockwise* direction. A
bus comes by each stop every 20 minutes.

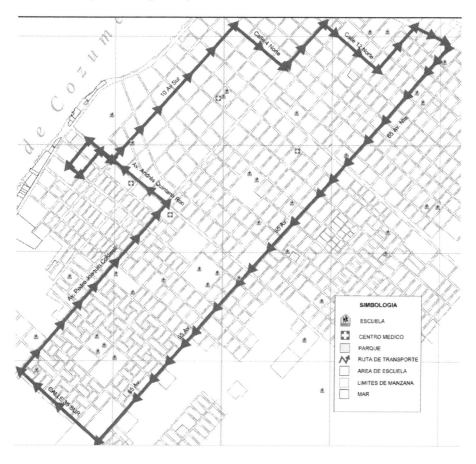

Uniper Bus Route 3 Chentuk (below) is serviced by Uniper bus #U25 and #U13, in a *counter-clockwise* direction. This bus stops by each stop every 20 minutes.

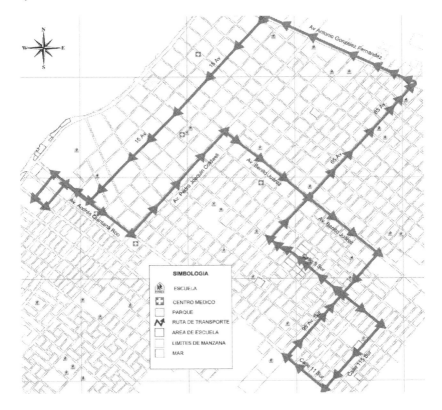

Uniper Bus Route 10 Huertas Familiares (below) is serviced by Uniper bus #U19 in a *counter-clockwise* direction. This bus stops by each stop every 45 minutes.

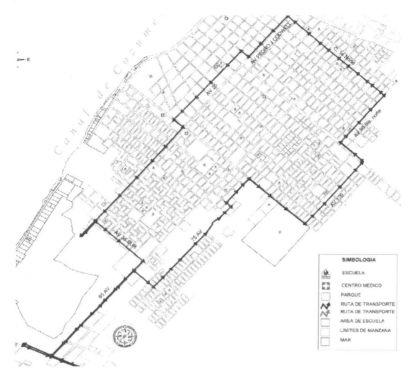

Uniper Bus Route 2 CTM-Flamingos (below) is serviced by Uniper buses #U21 and #T22, running in a counter clockwise direction. A bus comes by each stop every 15 minutes.

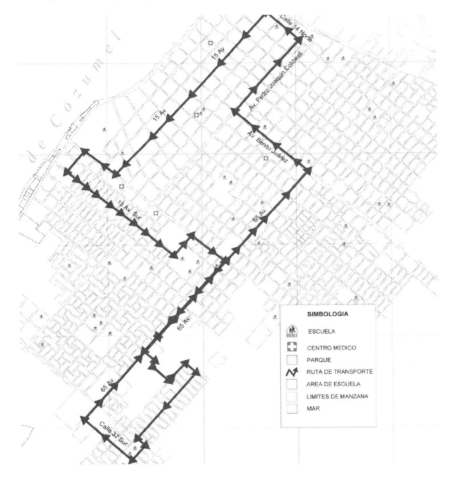

Uniper Route 4 Emiliano Zapata (below) is serviced by Uniper buses #U06 and #U12, running the route in a *clockwise* direction. A bus stops at each stop every 15 minutes.

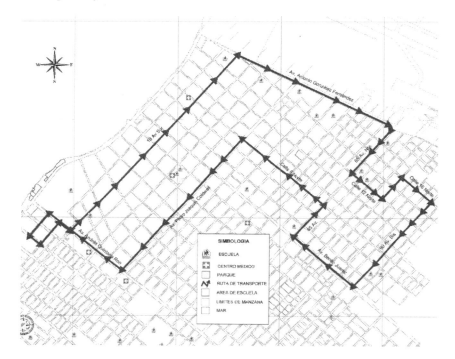

Uniper Route 11 Fincas (below) is run by Uniper bus #U10 in a *clockwise* direction and passes by each stop on its route every 55 minutes.

Uniper Route 13 Altamar-Miraflores (below) is run by Uniper bus #U23 in a *counterclockwise* direction and passes by each stop on its route every 35 minutes.

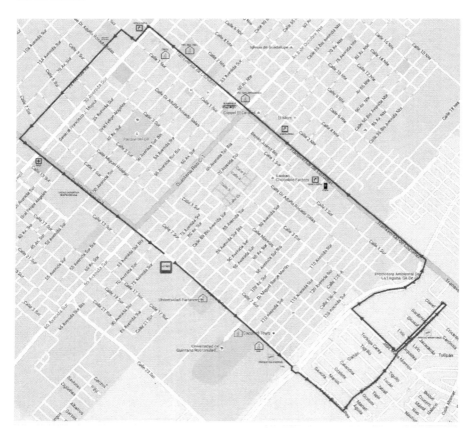

Uniper Route 14 Zamna-Taxistas (below) is run by Uniper bus #U23 in a *counterclockwise* direction and passes by each stop on its route every 35 minutes.

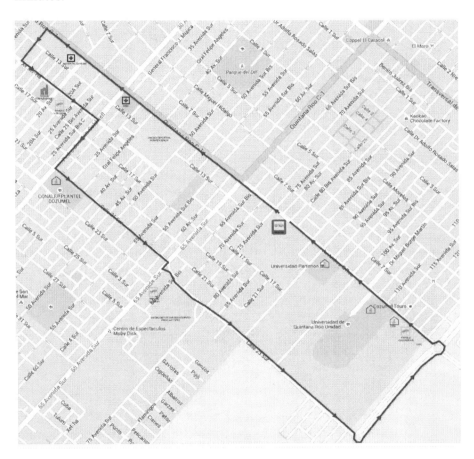

Taxis

Taxi rates in Cozumel are based on a rate sheet showing zones and point-to-point fares rather than taximeters. Each taxi driver has a laminated rate chart of two front-and-back pages that he will show you if you ask. They also offer bilingual guide services, island tours, limo service (14 pax Lincoln Navigator, 6 pax Lincoln Town car), 7 pax minivans, 14 pax vans, handicapped van service, 36 pax all-terrain truck-busses, and 45 pax a/c tour busses, as well as taxis. Call them at 987-872-1130 or 987-872-1167. Taxi office is located on Calle 2 between Avenidas 5 and 10. Email them at **taxicozumel@hotmail.com**

Commercial and private aviation

All commercial flights leave from Cozumel's International Airport (CZM). The phones at the airport general office are 872-2081 and 872-0485.

Private planes may take off and land at the new aerodrome Capt. Eduardo Toledo south of town at KM 11.2 (200 25' 31.2" N 870 00' 5.3" W), but if their flight originated outside of Mexico, they will need to land at another Mexican airport first to clear customs and immigration as there is no facility at the aerodrome to get this done. They also offer flying classes. The runway is 11/29, 1.2 KM, paved. For more info, call them at (987) 100-9829, or see their website **www.fly2cozumel.com.mx** or email them at **info@fly2cozumel.com.mx**

National flights

Mayair operates a local daily service to and from Cancun, as well as flights from Cancun to Merida, Villahermosa, and Veracruz. For current schedule, see **www.mayair.com.mx** or call them at (987) 872-3609. They have a discount plan (plan local) for residents.

Interjet is a national airline that flies from the CZM international terminal to Mexico City, see **www.interjet.com.mx** or call 01-800-011-2345

International Flights

Several international airline companies service Cozumel with flights originating from the US and Canada. Many more international airline companies service Cancun's airport, and it is relatively easy to connect with these Cancun flights from Cozumel via ferry and bus or taxi rides, or by taking a commuter flight from Cozumel to Cancun.

Airlines with offices in the Cozumel airport

American **www.aa.com** 01-800-904-6000

Air Canada **www.aircanada.com** 01 800 719 2827

Continental/United **www.continental.com** 01-800-900-5000
Delta **www.delta.com** 01-800-123-4710

Frontier **www.frontierairlines.com** 01-800-432-1359 (international call)

Sun Country **www.suncountry.com** 01 800-924-6184 (International call)

US Airways **www.usairways.com** 01-800-902-2100 (International call)

WestJet **www.westjet.com** 01-800-514-7288

Air charters

Ferinco flies air charters from the general aviation side of the terminal. For prices and schedules, call 01-987-872-1781 to reach their office on Av. Pedro Joaquin Coldwell at Calle 5.

Bus lines on the mainland

To find out schedules or to buy tickets for bus lines ADO, OCC, ATS, Mayab, or Riviera Airport Shuttle that service the mainland, stop by one of the two ADO bus ticket offices on Calle 2 near AV. 10 or Av. 10 between Juarez and Calle 1 sur in Cozumel, or call them at (987) 869-2553.

Chapter 23
PRIVATE TRANSPORTATION

Mexican driver's license

To find out how to obtain a Mexican driver's license, see the section entitled **OTHER DOCUMENTS.**

Registering a foreign-plated vehicle

If your vehicle had valid foreign plates when it entered Mexico with you, you do not need to keep the foreign plates current or register the vehicle in Mexico in any way. Bear in mind, however, you must have a current inspection sticker and plates to drive it back into the US or Canada, or you will be liable to be ticketed there. As long as your visa is current, your car is legal in Mexico. See the section on importing a vehicle into Mexico for more rules. You cannot buy a foreign plated vehicle from another foreigner inside of Mexico. You both must leave Mexico along with the car and re-title it outside of Mexico before you re-import it under your name. If you buy a used vehicle in Mexico, be aware that many flood-damaged and stolen cars find their way south of the border.

Buying and registering a Mexican vehicle

You can buy a car in Mexico and register it with Mexican plates if you have a *Residente Temporal* or *Residente Permanente* visa. However, be aware that there is a hefty yearly state ownership tax *(tenencia)* associated with Mexican titled vehicles. The tax is based on the value of the car and its age. It is highest the first few years and then it drops down each year until the vehicle is ten years old, after which, it is forgiven. In Quintana Roo, this tax expired in 2012. One of the advantages to buying a Mexican car is that the repair parts are readily available. One disadvantage is that you cannot bring a Mexican vehicle back to the US or Canada (except for short visits) without a lot of time and expense to bring it up to the standards demanded by US and Canada Customs, and for many vehicles, this is impossible.

Vehicle liability insurance

Vehicle liability insurance is required by law in Cozumel. If you have foreign plates, most Mexican insurance companies do not require the foreign plates to be current. Be sure the Mexican auto insurance coverage you purchase includes claims adjusters who will come to the scene of an accident, that it will provide legal representation for you, and that it will post any necessary bonds or bail if you are jailed due to an accident. If you have an accident, it is illegal to move your vehicle and you may be detained by the police if anyone was hurt until fault can be established. Call your insurance immediately to have an adjuster sent to the scene. If you are required to go to jail until things are sorted out, have your insurance provider send you a legal representative. The law in Mexico is based on Napoleonic Code, which says you are guilty until proven innocent. Always carry in your car copies of your: proof of insurance, proof of ownership, driver's license, visa, Temporary Vehicle Import Permit, and if it has been over 180 days since you imported the vehicle, a copy of the law that states that as long as your visa is current your temporary vehicle import permit is exempt.

Some Mexican auto insurance providers:

www.mexinsure.com
www.mexpro.com
www.hdimexicaninsurance.com
www.mapfre.com

Overstaying the Temporary Vehicle Import Permit period of 180 days

Article 106 of the Mexican Importation Law says that your car is legal in Mexico so long as your visa is valid, regardless of whether or not your foreign plates or foreign registration are expired, or your Temporary Vehicle Import Permit's 180 days have passed. This means that if you have an *Residente Permanente* visa or a *Residente Temporal* visa and keep it renewed each year, you can keep your foreign-plated car in Mexico and simply keep extending your permit period indefinitely as long as you keep the *Aduana* informed of your current visa status (see below on how to do this). However, if you leave Mexico with your car after the initial 180 days, you must turn in the permit and sticker at the border when you leave and buy a new permit when you return.

Text of Article 106 (keep a copy of this in your car)

Legislación Federal (Vigente al 28 de enero de 2011)
LEY ADUANERA
TITULO CUARTO REGIMENES ADUANEROS
CAPITULO III. TEMPORALES DE IMPORTACION Y DE EXPORTACION.
SECCION PRIMERA. IMPORTACIONES TEMPORALES.

I.- DISPOSICIONES GENERALES.

ARTICULO 106. SE ENTIENDE POR REGIMEN DE IMPORTACION TEMPORAL, LA ENTRADA AL PAIS DE MERCANCIAS PARA PERMANECER EN EL POR TIEMPO LIMITADO Y CON UNA FINALIDAD ESPECIFICA, SIEMPRE QUE RETORNEN AL EXTRANJERO EN EL MISMO ESTADO, POR LOS SIGUIENTES PLAZOS:

IV. POR EL PLAZO QUE DURE SU CALIDAD MIGRATORIA, INCLUYENDO SUS PRORROGAS, EN LOS SIGUIENTES CASOS:

A) LAS DE VEHICULOS PROPIEDAD DE EXTRANJEROS QUE SE INTERNEN AL PAIS CON CALIDAD DE INMIGRANTES RENTISTAS O DE NO INMIGRANTES, EXCEPTO TRATANDOSE DE REFUGIADOS Y ASILADOS POLITICOS, SIEMPRE QUE SE TRATE DE UN SOLO VEHICULO. LOS VEHICULOS QUE IMPORTEN TURISTAS Y VISITANTES LOCALES, INCLUSO QUE NO SEAN DE SU PROPIEDAD Y SE TRATE DE UN SOLO VEHICULO. OS VEHICULOS PODRAN SER CONDUCIDOS EN TERRITORIO NACIONAL POR EL IMPORTADOR, SU CONYUGE, SUS ASCENDIENTES, DESCENDIENTES O HERMANOS, AUN CUANDO ESTOS NO SEAN EXTRANJEROS, POR UN EXTRANJERO QUE TENGA ALGUNA DE LAS CALIDADES MIGRATORIAS A QUE SE REFIERE ESTE INCISO, O POR UN NACIONAL, SIEMPRE QUE EN ESTE ULTIMO CASO, VIAJE

A BORDO DEL MISMO CUALQUIERA DE LAS PERSONAS AUTORIZADAS PARA CONDUCIR EL VEHICULO Y PODRAN EFECTUAR ENTRADAS Y SALIDAS MULTIPLES.

How to extend a Temporary Vehicle Import Permit

Within 10 days after renewing your *Residente Temporal,* changing to a *Residente Permanente* visa, or converting from a *Visitante* visa to one of those two, you need to notify the Customs *(Aduana)* that you want to extend your Temporary Vehicle Import Permit. You do not need to go back to the border to do this; you can do it by mail or in person at the *Aduana* office. There is no fee. You will not be given a new sticker or registration papers, so be sure to keep a copy of the letter in your car. This is the letter you should prepare and present to the *Aduana*:

Por medio de la presente, me permito informarle a usted que El Instituto Nacional de Migración de este país me ha concedido prorroga en mi calidad migratoria por el tiempo de (number of days in your new visa) *días para permanecer en México, con vencimiento del día* (the date the visa expires). *Lo que estoy avisando a esta autoridad para los efectos del Articulo 106, fracción IV, inciso a de la Ley Aduanera, con respecto a la importacióntemporal de mi vehículo:*

- *Marca:* (make of vehicle),
- *Modelo:*(model),
- *No de serie:* (VIN number),
- *Efectuada por la Aduana de* (town original permit was granted),
- *Amparo del Permiso de Importación Temporal No.* (number on the holographic sticker),
- *Fecha de Entrada del vehículo:* (date of your entry with the vehicle),
- *Fecha de Vencimiento del Permiso:* (original expiration date of the permit)

Para que pueda prolongarse el plazo del vehículo mientras dure mi calidad migratoria.

Atentamente,
(Your signature)
(Your name)
(Date)

Mail the letter (certified) plus a copy of your new visa and a copy of the temporary vehicle import permit to:

Administración General de Aduanas
Administración Central de Planeación Aduanera
Av. Hidalgo No. 77, Módulo IV, primer piso
Col. Guerrero, Delegación Cuauhtémoc
Código Postal 06300, México, D.F.

If you cannot return the vehicle before the temporary import permit expires

So, what do you do if you simply <u>cannot</u> return your vehicle to the US before the Temporary Import Permit expires, and you are not eligible to keep it under the circumstances listed above? First, <u>do not drive it inside of Mexico after the expiration date of the permit</u>. Park it and file a request called a *Retorno Seguro* with:

Administración de Normatividad Internacional de la Administración General de Grandes Contribuyentes
Hidalgo #77, Módulo III, Planta Baja,
Colonia Guerrero, Delegación Cuauhtémoc, 06300, México, DF

Their phone numbers in DF are 58-02-22-82, 58-02-22-58, & 58-02-00-00.

This *Retorno Seguro*, once granted, will allow you a window of up to five days to drive your vehicle out of the country.

What if the vehicle was stolen? You must take the police report containing the vehicle's description, including the VIN number, make, and model, to the *Aduana* office closest to you and pay the import taxes that would have been due had you imported the vehicle in order to sell it. If you fail to do this, you will never be able to bring another vehicle into Mexico again with a Temporary Vehicle Permit.

What if the vehicle was in an accident and is not repairable? You have 5 days from the day after the accident to visit the *Aduana* closest to you and give them the accident report, a letter from the insurance adjuster saying the vehicle was written off as a total loss, and then must sign over the title of the vehicle and allow the *Aduana* to take possession of the remains so they can do with it as they see fit.

You can then call INFOSAT at 01-800-46-36-728 (within Mexico) or 1-877-448-8728 (from the US or Canada) to find out what hoops you have to jump through next to get the old Temporary Import Permit cancelled!

Authorized drivers

Section IV of Article 106 says the vehicle can be driven in Mexico by the owner/importer, the owner's spouse, their parents and grandparents, their decedents, their brothers or sisters, or by a foreigner who has the same immigration category as the owner. A Mexican citizen may only drive the vehicle when one of these previously mentioned authorized drivers is in the vehicle.

Selling a foreign-plated vehicle

Foreign-plated vehicles imported by their owners cannot be sold in Mexico, to anyone, under any circumstances, unless the vehicle is first nationalized. You can do this by going to a customs broker and have him convert your Temporary Vehicle Import Permit in to a Permanent Importation of the vehicle through the *Aduana*, paying the importation taxes, the *tenencia* tax, and re-plating the car with Mexican plates.

Traffic flow

The streets in Cozumel are shared by a sometimes-bewildering mix of cars, trucks, motorcycles, bicycles, tricycles, horse-drawn buggies, and many, weird, home-made combinations of a couple of these conveyances. The secret is to drive carefully and slowly. Being passed on the right is not an unusual event, nor is finding the vehicle in front of you is going to stop a while in the middle of the street while the driver makes a quick run into a nearby store or office. Taxis have an agenda all their own; it is always a good policy to give them a wide berth. Patience is the secret.

Traffic lights

Traffic signals in Cozumel also have their own idiosyncrasies. Unlike the US, where the sequence is green-yellow-red, here in Mexico the sequence is green-flashing green-yellow-red. Like many parts of the world, if the way is clear, a right turn is allowed here at a red light after a full stop. In most places in the world, the lights facing the south-bound traffic are synchronized to be the same color as that facing the north-bound traffic, unless there are secondary lights in place that regulate left turns. Here in Cozumel, the green light only appears on one side of the signal at a time, resulting in a situation where each lane at the intersection must wait for their own green light to continued straight or to turn left.

Things that slow traffic flow

Since the Cozumel police do not use radar, they have (like the rest of Mexico) found that strategically placed speed bumps *(topes)* and raised pedestrian crossing platforms *(plataformas)* do just about as well as slowing down traffic. The bumps (some of which are quite abrupt, and can cause serious damage when taken at speed) are all marked with signs indicating their presence.

Traffic laws

To drive a car in Mexico you must have a current, valid driver's license, either from your home country, or a Mexican license. To find out how to get a Mexican driver's license, see the section entitled **OTHER DOCUMENTS.** If you are driving your own vehicle, you need to have on hand at all times copies of: the vehicle registration, proof of ownership (title), your passport, your visa, and proof of insurance. If your vehicle was imported temporarily into Mexico, you also need the holographic sticker on the windshield, a copy of the import permit (and a copy of the letter to the *Aduana* showing you have extended your visa if the initial 180 days of the permit has passed) and a copy of Article 106 of the *Ley Aduanera* (see above for text of the law).

Helmet law

Everyone, regardless of age, is required to wear a helmet in Cozumel while driving or riding a motorized, two wheeled vehicle. No more than two people are allowed to ride on one motorcycle or moped at the same time.

Seat belts

Use of seat belts is mandatory in both front and back seats.

Calles and *Avenidas*

Avenidas (which usually go north –south) have right of way, *Calles* (which always go each-west) do not. The exceptions are the Avenidas Xelha, Andres Quintana Roo, and Antonio Gonzalez Fernandez, which all run east-west and still have the right-of-way. Calle Benito Juarez from Avenida Pedro Joaquín Coldwell eastward has no stop signs and has the right-of-way.

Traffic circles

When arriving at a traffic circle, the vehicle already inside the circle has right-of-way. However, in common practice on Cozumel, this rule is not always observed at all traffic circles; some they do and some they don't!

Stops for traffic violations

If you are stopped for a moving violation, the police officer is not authorized to issue a ticket for traffic violations or settle the fine on the spot. He will take your license with him to the police station and request that you go to the station to resolve the infraction and retrieve your license. At the station, you can plead your case or pay the fine.

Parking downtown

Parking is at a premium in downtown San Miguel, and street-side parking spots are not always easy to find deeper in town either. There are many privately operated parking lots that help make up for this lack of street-side parking. They are clearly marked with signs saying "Parking" or *"Estacimiento."* If the sign also says *"Solo Pensionados,"* that means the lot is for monthly or yearly subscription only. If a lot says *"Parking Privado,"* that means it is a private lot, not for public hire. All lots that charge for parking have attendants who will show you where to park and accept your cash payment. Most close and chain the lot at 9 PM. Some of the larger businesses like Mega, Chedraui, Punta Langosta Mall, and others have free parking lots for their patrons.

Parking on Av. Rafael E. Melgar (the *malecón*) is the most tightly controlled. There is no public parking allowed on the malecon weekdays and Saturdays from 9AM until 6PM. Taxi Only parking spaces are the space between the signs with the word *"TAXI PRINCIPA"* (meaning "starts here") and the words *"TAXI TERMINA"* (meaning "ends here"). Handicapped Only parking areas also exist, with signs showing the international sign of a wheelchair. Horse drawn buggies have special parking areas on the *malecón* marked by signs with the image of horse-drawn buggy on them, indicating where the buggy parking starts and where it ends.

Parking violations

Curbs painted **yellow** are for short term (less than ten minutes) parking. When the pavement has an **"E"** in a circle with a diagonal line through it, there is no parking on that part of the street. The bays let into the right hand sidewalks at intervals along the downtown *calles* between Av. 10 and the *malecón* are for short-term (less than 10 minutes) parking only. Curbs painted **red** are *No Parking* zones. A round sign with a diagonal line across a capital **E** means no parking. Round signs with the word *Taxi* and an arrow mean only taxi parking from this point to the next sign with the word Taxi on it. Bus stops are no parking areas and are signed with the word *Autobus* or *Parada* (bus stop). Many driveways are marked *no parking, vado,* or *vado permanente,* and blocking one of these will get you towed. The sign in front of schools that reads *Momentaneo Maximo 10 minutos* means stopping and waiting in your car is allowed for only ten minutes. Parking within a car length of an intersection is illegal, and will get you towed faster than anything else. If your vehicle is found illegally parked, it may be either towed to the police storage compound or the license plates may be removed by the patrolman. If your plates are removed, you need to go directly to the police station and pay the fine before they will be returned. If you are found driving without plates, you will be jailed.

Towed, Impounded vehicles

To retrieve a towed vehicle from police impound, you will need to bring proof of ownership (title), proof of insurance, your passport, driver's license, visa, (*Tarjeta de circulación* if the car is registered in Mexico),

Temporary Vehicle Import Permit (and letter extending the permit period, if appropriate) with you when you go to pay the fine.

Police Station

The police station in Cozumel is located next to the *Palacio Municipal* at Av. Xelha and Calle Gonzalo Guerrero. Phone (987) 872-0409

Gasoline

Pemex is the only brand of gas sold in Mexico. The types of gasoline offered are *Magna* (green pump, unleaded, 87 octane), *Premium* (red pump, unleaded, 93 octane) and *Diesel* (black pump). There is no self-service and tipping is customary, but a couple of pesos will do. VISA and MasterCard are accepted. Be sure the pump is set on "0" before the attendant begins pumping gas into your car.

Rental vehicles and motor-scooters

Bear in mind when renting a moto or vehicle, the laws concerning accidents are very different here in Mexico than they are in the US or Canada. For one, the law in Mexico is based on *Roman Law* (Civil Law, or Napoleonic Law) and not *Common Law* (English Law) like the US. This means that in Mexican law you are guilty until proven innocent. Consequently, if you have an accident where there is any property damage or bodily harm caused, you will be held at the police station until your insurance agrees to pay for the damages, or a settlement with the injured party is resolved and the amount agreed upon paid in full. Although Mexican law does not provide a way for injured parties to claim restitution for "pain and suffering," they are able to sue for lost wages. Most insurance policies issued with Cozumel rental contracts do not cover this aspect of damages. Some do not cover much of anything at all. Read you contract carefully and have it explained to you if you do not understand it.

Chapter 24
MEDICAL

Reciprocal agreements covering foreign-government sponsored health care plans

If you are accustomed to government provided health care (as in Canada), be aware that Mexico does not have a reciprocal agreement with any country for health care services. Health services provided in Mexico are not covered under the US Medicare system, either.

A few tips before getting into doctors, hospitals and insurance:

* Wash your vegetables, fruits, and counter tops with tap water that has chlorine (*cloro*) added at the ratio of 20 drops to 1 gallon of water.
* Drink bottled water and use bottled water to make ice to avoid contracting Giardia.
* Dengue fever is endemic to Cozumel, so use mosquito repellent in the evening and early morning to avoid becoming infected. Cozumel now also has Chikungunya and Zika, two other nasty mosquito-borne virus. Be sure to keep your property clear of standing water where mosquitoes can breed.
* Get your flu shot every year.

IMSS **insurance**

Low cost (under $300 USD per year; exact price depends on your age) *IMSS (Instituto Mexicano del Seguro Social)* medical insurance is available to *Residente Temporal* or *Residente Permanente* visa holders. All medical care and tests are covered by your annual premium with no deductible or co-pay. Prescription medicines are provided free of charge, but not all of the newest drugs are available through the *IMSS* system. There are three ways to apply. The first is if you are an employee, you can apply under your company's policy. If that is the case, all you need is you passport, visa, and company's *IMSS* number. If you are applying for individual insurance, you need copies of your passport, visa, proof of Mexican residency (utility bill, etc.), and two *infantile* pictures. If you are applying for family coverage, you will need the birth certificates, marriage license (if you have a spouse as a dependent), and two *infantile* pictures of each dependent. The birth certificates and marriage license need to have an *apostile* (see the section on **VISAS** for details on how) and all documents need to be translated into Spanish by an approved translator. Take all these items to the *"afiliación"* window at the *IMSS* hospital on Av. Quintana Roo during the last week of the month (inscriptions are only open on the first day of the month) and they will give you an application to fill out. Sometimes a physical exam is required, depending on the answers given on the application.

You will not be covered for pre-existing conditions including, but not limited to: Cancer, chronic diseases, kidney disease, heart disease, lung disease, neurological diseases, cerebrovascular disease, peripheral vascular disease, drug or alcohol dependency, psychiatric illnesses, HIV, AIDS, or traumatic muscular injury that continues to require treatment. Benefits are phased in over a three year period. For the first six months, benign breast tumors are not covered. Births are not covered for the first ten months. Also, during the first year certain surgeries are not covered. These are: Surgery for gynecological conditions other than cancer, surgery for vein disorders, surgery for sinuses, nose, hemorrhoids, rectal fistulas, tonsils, adenoids, hernias (except herniated discs), lithotripsy, or elective surgery. During the first two years, the following will not be covered: Orthopedic surgery, plastic surgery, eyeglasses, contacts, hearing aids, surgical correction of astigmatism, Lasik surgery or equivalent, treatment of self-inflicted injuries, preventive care, treatments for behavioral or psychiatric disorders, dental care, or infertility treatments. After your third year, everything is covered.

The drug benefit comes into play after the third year, but only covers drugs dispensed at *IMSS*. Many name-brand drugs are not offered at *IMSS,* but they are usually cheaper in Mexican pharmacies than in the US or Canada.

Seguro Popular

Another Mexican-government sponsored health plan available to *Residente Temporal* and *Residente Permanente* visa holders who are not enrolled in *IMSS* is the *Centro de Salud's Seguro Popular*. Take your passport, visa, proof of residence (light, phone, or water bill), and copies of each to the *Seguro Popular* office across the street from the emergency entrance of the Cozumel General Hospital on calle 13 at Av. 20 and fill out the application. The cost is based on a sliding scale depending on your income, but is around 1,200 pesos per year. See **www.seguro-popular.gob.mx** for more info.

Pay as you go

Paying for medical care out of pocket is not nearly as expensive in Mexico as the US. Doctor visits can be as little as $10 USD, and drugs, especially generic drugs, are very inexpensive.

Private insurance

There are also many private insurance companies offering health insurance to expats living in Mexico, including: GNP **www.gnp.com.mx** and MetLife **www.metlife.com.mx**

Air medivac services

If you prefer to have emergency medical procedures performed in your home country, there are air medivac policies available from several companies, including:
Medical Air Services **www.medairservices.com**
SkyMed **www.skymed.com**
Medjet Assist **www.medjetassist.com**

Red Cross emergency services

On Cozumel, the *Cruz Roja Mexicana* (Mexican Red Cross) provides the ambulance service for all accidents and medical emergencies, free of charge. The ambulances also carry paramedics to provide first aid assistance, also free of charge. They will take you to the hospital or clinic of your choice. Their 24 hour emergency number is **065.** They also offer walk-in emergency patient care. In addition, *Cruz Roja* now offers low-cost medical consultations, physical exams, lab work, and injections. A pediatrician, dentist, and general practitioner are available between 9 AM and 9 PM as well as trained nurses and technicians. They have an infirmary and nursing staff for patients who need overnight observation, treatment or recovery, and provide patients with free prescription medicines as available. Diabetic patients may come in daily to self-check blood sugar and to receive insulin. *Cruz Roja* is now in the process of training all of Cozumel's lifeguards to be paramedics. They are located at Av. 65 at the corner of Calle 25 Sur. Their office phone is 869-0698, VHF: channel 16, CB: channel 9, Email: **xroja@prodigy.net**, **www.cruzrojacozumel.org**.

Private ambulance services

There are several private ambulance services operating in Cozumel. Be aware that they are not free and will only take you to the hospital they work for; they will not take you to the hospital of your choice.

DIF (Desarrollo Integral de Familia)

This government agency charged with the development of infants and families offers many services to the public. They have classes on nutrition, parenting, and managing diabetes and other illnesses. They also periodically offer vision tests, auditory tests, mammograms, etc. See their website at **www.difcozumel.gob.mx,** or go by their main office at Av. 30 between Calles 37 & 39, Col. San Miguel II, (987) 857-2300 / 857-2301

Other hospitals and clinics in Cozumel

IMSS Av. 11 & Av. Pedro Joaquin Coldwell 872-0639
International Hospital Calle 5 Sur between Av. Melgar and Av.5, phone 872-1430, or 872-2387, fax 872-1848. They have a hyperbaric chamber.
Clinica Medica San Miguel Calle 6 Norte between Av. 5 and 10, phone 872-0103, 6155, 5850, or 3241. This clinic also has a hyperbaric chamber.
Centro de Salud (Public Health Center at the General Hospital) Calle 11 Sur & Av. 20 Sur. Equipped with a hyperbaric chamber.
Centro Medico Cozumel/Grupo Costamed, Calle 1 Sur between Av. 50 and Av.50bis, phone 872-9400, 24-hrs
Cozumel General Hospital, Av. Quintana Roo between Av. 10 & 20 phone 872-5182
IslaMed, Calle Salas between Av. 85 & 85 bis, phone 869-6171

Chapter 25
COMUNICATIONS

Land-line phones

The Mexican phone company (Telmex), offers a package that includes a high-speed DSL with wireless modem (which they call 'Infinitum') as well as a telephone land line. With this service you can use both the phone and internet simultaneously. The Telmex package also includes free world-wide long distance , except, oddly enough, the "toll-free" US 800 numbers! To contract phone service, go to the Telmex office at Adolfo Rosado Salas #9 (between Av. 5 and 10) with your passport and proof of Mexican residency (a power bill, lease agreement, deed, or letter from your landlord. Phone bills are due monthly. They are open Monday through Friday 8 AM to 2 PM, and they have a 24 hour automated payment machine out front. If your bill does not arrive on time, Telmex will not accept that as a reason not to pay on time and they will cut your service right after the due date passes. You can pay your bill at the Telmex office, any bank, the checkout of most supermarkets, or at any *OXXO* store up until two days before the bill is due. After that, you can only pay at the Telmex office.

To report a loss of service, call 050. For customer service about billing, call 01-800-123-0000. To contract new phone service, call 872-0910.

Wireless Internet service

You can contract pre-paid internet service via a wireless USB device that works throughout Mexico through the company Telcel. One of their agencies is TelyCom, located at #508 Av Pedro J. Coldwell between Calle 5 and Hidalgo. They can be reached at 872-7514 or **www.telcel.com** The USB device costs around $650 pesos and comes with 30 days of usage (up to 3 gigabytes) included in the package. More time can be purchased either at one of their agencies' offices or over the internet with your credit card. Time blocks of 1, 5, 15, or 30 days are available. Packages offering 10 gigabytes of usage per month are also available for a higher rate. You can also contract monthly Internet service through a six-month minimum contract with Telcel, or with the cable company Cablemás.

Cable TV and Land-line Internet providers

Cable de Cozumel   989 6303
Cablemás 872-2253

Satellite TV providers

Dishnetwork **www.dishnetwork.com**
DirecTV **www.directv.com**
Star Choice **www.starchoice.com.mx**
Sky TV 872-3898 **www.sky.mx**

Satellite radio
Both XM and Sirius work in Cozumel.

Broadcast TV
None available

VoIP providers
Skype, Magic Jack, Vonage, and many others are VoIP (Voice over Internet Protocol) services you can subscribe to for making and receiving international calls inexpensively through your computer over your DSL connection.

Free Wi-Fi hot spots
Many stores, restaurants, bars and hotels have free Wi-Fii. They are also found on the ferries and at the airport.

Outgoing emails from Wi-Fi locations
In an attempt to prevent spam, Telmex and other Mexican service providers running Wi-Fi spots have blocked Port 25, the port most commonly used by Outlook, Windows Mail, Thunderbird, or Entourage. Incoming messages on the email programs are not blocked since they commonly use Port 110, but outgoing emails will never leave your outbox. To get around this blockage, use a mail service like Yahoo or Hotmail through your web browser.

Incoming calls from the US made with pre-paid calling cards

Some pre-paid calling cards issued in the US and Canada are not accepted by the Mexican telephone company and so calls attempted by someone with one of those cards will not be connected. If you have someone outside Mexico that has been trying to call your Mexican phone number without success, this may be the reason.

Cell phones

Cell phones in Cozumel come in two varieties: Pre-paid and contracted service. The contracted phone has lower rates, but to have the contracted service you must have an address in Mexico. The pre-paid phones come with a few minutes included, but you must purchase more minutes as you go and they expire after a set amount of time if you do not use them in that period. If you keep your pre-paid Telcel phone (aka *"plan amigo"*) for more than a year, you can take it back to the provider and they will give you a new, lower rate that is cheaper than the contracted plan.

GSM and CDMA

Both GSM and CDMA phones on the 1900 band work on Cozumel.

US cell phone service providers with Mexico plans other than roaming

Verizon (Mexico plan)
AT&T (WorldConnectMexico plan)
Nextel

Mexican cell phone service providers in Cozumel

Movistar **www.movistar.com.mx**
Telcel **www.telcel.com**
AT&T **www.att.com.mx**
Iusacell **www.iusacell.com.mx**
Nextel **www.nextel.com.mx**

Contracting a Mexican cell phone service

When you go to buy your cell phone in Cozumel, you will need to take your passport with you. The sales person will make a copy and fax it to their main office, who will then send it on to the government. It will take about 48 hours after the passport has been faxed for the cell phone to be ready to activate.

Registering your cell phone

All cell phones in Mexico are required to be registered with *RENAUT (Registro Nacional de Usuarios de Telefonía Móvil)* at **www.renaut.gob.mx** To register your phone after it has already been purchased, send the following text message to 2877: ALTA.your given name.your family name.your birthdate (dd/mm/yyyy). For example: ALTA.John.Smith.03121970 If you have a *CURP* number (see the section on **OTHER DOCUMENTS** for more info), you can send your *CURP* instead of your name and birth date. If you are purchasing a new phone, you can register it at the point of purchase with your passport and visa. If you ever lose your phone, it is important to report it to the police as stolen as soon as possible and get an incident report from them to cover you in case the phone is subsequently used in a crime.

Dialing

To call a Cozumel cell phone number from a Cozumel land-line phone, dial 044 + the area code (987) + the 7 digit phone number.

To call a long distance cell phone from a land-line phone dial 045 + the area code + the 7 digit phone number.

To call long-distance to a land-line from a land line within Mexico, dial 01 + area-code + the 7-digit phone number.

To call a local land line number from a local land line number you need dial only the last 7 digits.

To call any land line from a cell phone, dial the area code + the last 7 digits.

To call any local cell phone from any local cell phone, you need dial only the last 7 digits.

To call any long-distance cell phone from any local cell phone, dial the area code + the last 7 digits.

Direct-dialed international calls are made by dialing 00 plus the country code (Us and Canada are 00+1) plus the area code plus the 7 digit number. Operator assisted international calls are made by calling the international operator at 090.

The area code in Cozumel is 987.
The country code for Mexico is 52.
The country code for US and Canada is 001

Calling Mexico from the US or Canada

To dial a Mexican land-line phone from outside Mexico, dial 011 + 52 +area code + last 7 digits.

To dial a Mexican cell phone from outside Mexico, dial 011 + 52 + 1 + area code + 7-digit number.

Toll free numbers and 900 numbers

Mexican phone numbers with the 800 prefix are toll-free within Mexico, but calling a U.S. toll-free number from Mexico costs the same as an overseas call.

To call a US 800 number, dial 001-880 and the last seven digits.
To call a US 844 number, dial 001-885 and the last seven digits.
To call a US 866 number, dial 001-883 and the last seven digits.
To call a US 885 number, dial 001-884 and the last seven digits.
To call a US 887 number, dial 001-882 and the last seven digits.
To call a US 888 number, dial 001-881 and the last seven digits.

These calls will not be toll-free, but you will be connected.

900 prefix numbers cannot be called from Mexico.

Public Phones

Calls from public phones can be made with a pre-paid Telmex phone card *(Tarjeta Ladtel)* or a less expensive, off- brand phone card *(Tarjeta para llamadas de larga distancia de descuento)* available at most convenience stores.   You can also add more minutes to these cards by accessing the website noted on the card and paying by credit card online.   Calls to the USA and Canada are very inexpensive using the card-phones.   Public phones advertising foreign calls using your credit card will charge much more because of their high connection fee plus high per-minute charges.

Chapter 26
MAIL & DELIVERY SERVICES

Postal Service *(Correos Mexicanos)*

The Mexican Postal Service offers several services to the postal patron, including home delivery, General Delivery, and Post Office boxes.

Home delivery

If you have a mail box, the mailman will leave your mail in it. Otherwise, he will try to stuff it under your front door. If he is trying to deliver a letter or package that requires a signature, he will blow a distinctive whistle while at the curb so that if you are home, you will come outside and sign for the delivery.

Post office location and hours

The post office is located on Av. Melgar at Calle 7. The phone number is (987) 872-0106. It is open weekdays from 9 A.M. to 4 P.M. and Saturdays from 9 A.M. to 1 P.M. It is closed on Sundays and federal holidays.

General Delivery

To sign up to receive mail in care of General Delivery at the Post Office, you need to show your ID and sign in at the front desk. Any letters you are to receive there must be addressed:

Lista de Correos
(your name)
Cozumel, Quintana Roo
Mexico, 77600

A clip board hanging at the front desk has a list of all incoming General Delivery mail. General Delivery mail will be returned to sender if not claimed within 10 days.

P.O. Boxes

To rent a P.O. box, bring a copy of your passport and a copy of a utility bill to the counter and fill out the application.

Cozumel zip codes

77600 P.O. boxes at main post office & Colonia Centro

77610 Base Area

77613 Zona Hotelera Norte

77620 Colonia Emiliano Zapata, Colonia Felix Gonzalez Canto

77622 Colonia 10 de Abril

77640 Colonia Adolfo Lopez Mateos

77642 Colonia Cuzamil (INVIQROO)

77645 Colonia San Gervasio 1 & 2, Colonia Chen Tuk, & Colonia Repobladores de 1848

77660 Colonia Maravilla, Colonia Magisterio, & Colonia Independencia

77663 Colonia Colonos Cuzamil & Colonia Andrés Quintana Roo (formerly known as Colonia Gonzalo Guerrero)

77665 Colonia San Miguel 1

77666 Fraccionamiento Flores Magon 3, Fraccionamientos San Miguel 2 & 3 & Golondrinas 1 & 2, Colonia CTM, Colonia FOVISSTE, Colonia Flamingos 1 & 2, Colonia Taxistas

77670 Colonia Flores Magon 1 & 2, Colonia Naval, Colonia Juan Bautista de la Vega, INFONAVIT Cozumel Turistico, Zona Industrial

77673 Colonia Ixchel & Colonia Huertas Familiares

77675 Zona Hotelera Sur

Delivery services *(paqueterias* or *mensajerias)*

Estafeta Av. 15 x Calles 2 & 4 norte (987)872-4270

Logex 25 sur x Av. 50 & Calle 8, (987) 872-6833

Multipack Av. 25 between Calle 2 & 4

PakMail (& Dypaq) Av. 10 between Juarez & Calle 1, (987) 872-3676

Papago Express Juarez between Av. 50 & 55

DHL Calle 6 between Melgar & Av 5, 1-800-765-6345

CDY Calle 1 between Av. 20 & 25

FedEx Av. Andres Q. Roo between Av. Melgar and Av. 10, 987-2631

Cozumel Colonias

1. Centro
2. 10 de Abril
3. Emiliano Zapata
4. Adolfo Lopez Mateos
5. Cuzamil (INVIQROO)
6. Flores Magon (INVIQROO)
7. Repobladores de 1848
8. Chen Tuk
9. Juan Bautista De la Vega
10. San Gervasio 1 &2
11. Maravilla
12. Indepencia
13. Andres Quintana Roo
   (formerly Gonzalo Guerrero)
14. San Miguel 1
15. San Miguel 2
16. Flamingos 1 &2
17. Taxistas
18. C.T.M.
19. Zona Industrial

20. Huertas Familiares
21. Colonos Cuzamil
22. Zona Hotel Sur
23. Zona Hotel Norte
24. Felix Gonzalez Canto
25. Magisterio
26. Ixchel
27. FOVISSSTE
28. Cozumel Turistico
29. Naval
30. Golondrinas 1 &2
31. Base Area

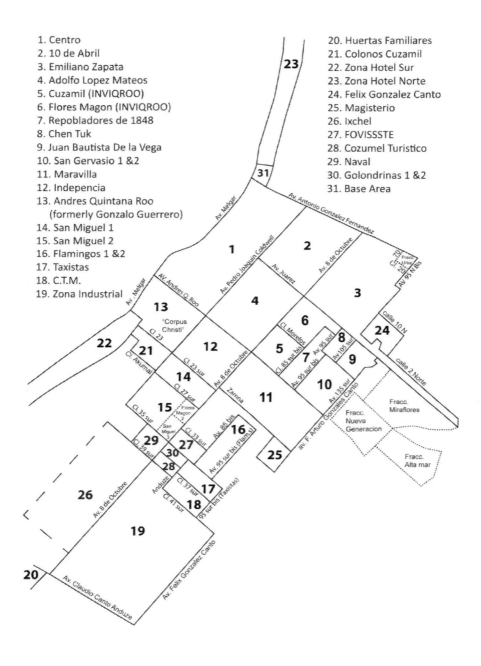

Chapter 27
MEDIA

Cozumel Radio Stations
98.1 FM XHPYA Riviera FM
89.9 FM XHRB Stereo Sol
810 AM XERB stereo Sol

Local newspapers

El Semanario de Cozumel is our weekly newspaper and has a web page at
www.elsemanariodecozumel.com

Novedades de Quintana Roo is a statewide newspaper but has a wrapper
that is Cozumel news.

Local TV stations and channels

PromoVision (Channel 10) Local news and programming
Canal 35, TV Coral
5TV (25 on cable)

Broadcast TV is not available in Cozumel

Internet radio

http://www.radiocoral.com/v2/ (also broadcast on canal 35 on cable)

http://cozumelradio.net/

Satellite radio
Both XM and Sirius work in Cozumel.

Cozumel oriented websites

www.EverythingCozumel.com (the publishers of this book)
www.cozumel.net
www.islacozumel.net
www.cometocozumel.com
www.cozumel.travel
www.cozumelmycozumel.com
www.thisiscozumel.com
www.viva-cozumel.com
www.cozumelmexico.net
www.gocozumel.com
www.ironmancozumel.com
www.cozumel4you.com

Chapter 28
YOUR HOME

Household help

Before hiring domestic help, be sure and read the section on **Employees.**
The average wage for a maid in Cozumel is 40 pesos per hour.

Handy men

Handy men are indispensable here on the island.   In cases where you
would call a plumber or an electrician in the states, here you will use a
handyman. Jacks of all trades (and often masters of none!) these guys will
know where to find a part that just might work to replace the old water-
heater part that is no longer made (or available on the island), how to figure
out why your air-conditioner keeps cutting off when you turn on the water,
or how to stop your water pump from losing prime and overheating all the
time. Just don't expect any of them to follow code! The best way to find
one of these fellows is to ask your neighbor for references and a phone
number.

Gardeners

Jardineros (gardeners) are another type of help you will probably need
while living here. They will know what plants work well here on Cozumel
(and which ones will do poorly), when and how much to trim back, and
best of all, they will carry off the trimmings, since the garbage collection
truck will not!

Alarm services

There are several security services here on the island, but be aware that
their alarms <u>are not</u> connected to the police station in any way.

Chapter 29
RENTING OUT YOUR
CONDO OR HOME

IVA tax on rent

If you rent out your Cozumel condo or home it is not subject to the Value Added Tax (*IVA*) as long as it is unfurnished and the renter is using it for non-commercial purposes. If the property is furnished, or the renter uses the property for commercial purposes, you must collect and remit *IVA*. You will need a Mexican attorney and accountant to set up your business in order to have an *RFC* number (Mexican Taxpayer account) so you can remit the taxes. See the section on **OTHER DOCUMENTS** for an explanation of an *RFC*.

Reporting your rental income to the SAT *(Servicio de Administracion Tributaria)*

Nonresident individuals are liable to tax on their Mexican-sourced income. Gross rental income from the leasing of real estate, property and time-sharing services by a nonresident individual is subject to a 25% withholding tax. No deductions are allowed. The *Servicio de Administracion Tributaria (SAT)* is responsible for assessment and collection. Non-Resident foreigners that are renting their homes out and are not reporting the income through a Mexican must pay a 25% tax on their rental income. No deductions are allowed.

Reporting rental income to the US IRS

The rent you receive from renting out property in Mexico is reportable to the US IRS if you are a US citizen as part of your world-wide income. If that property is in your *Fideicomiso* and you loan it out to a family member, you are liable for reporting the fair market value of the daily rent as a distribution from the *Fideicomiso* (IRC §643(i)(1), as amended by the 2010 HIRE Act). If the property is strictly a rental and you do not ever use it yourself more than 14 days a year, you can treat the home as a rental property for US IRS purposes and deduct much of the upkeep of the home.

Evicting a renter

Evicting a renter in Mexico can be very difficult if the signed rental contract was not written and recorded by a notary as a binding contract. Simply filling out a blank contract will not protect the property owner if the renter decides to stop paying rent. It may take up to a year or more to evict the tenant if the lease was not recorded by a notary.

Chapter 30
SHOPPING

Plan Locale, the discount plan for locals

Apply for this discount card at the *Modulo De Plan* just outside the offices of Mexican WaterJets on Av. 6 Norte between 10th and 15th. You need your original *Residente Temporal* or *Residente Permanente* visa, proof of residence in Cozumel (current cable, light, or water bill) and 100 pesos. Your picture will be taken and a card issued while you wait.

Senior discount card from *INAPAM (Instituto Nacional de Las Personas Adultas Mayores)*

You can get your senior discount card at *INAPAM* on the southwest corner of Av. 50 bis and Calle 3. You must be over 60 and have a *Residente Temporal* or *Residente Permanente* visa. Bring a copy of your visa, 2 copies of all pages of your passport, a copy of your utility bill, your *CURP* number, and 3 infantile photos. The card will get you discounts on property taxes, the ferries, Mayair fares, bus fares and medication, among other things.

Liquor laws

Alcoholic beverages may only be sold for take-away (grocery stores, liquor stores, etc.) between the hours of 9 AM and 9 PM, Monday through Saturday, and 9 AM to 3 PM on Sundays. A few convenience stores have special permits for after-hour sales.

Chapter 31
ART, CULTURE, & PARKS

Cozumel Library

Spanish language books are available from the municipal Library on Avenida Pedro Joaquín Coldwell at Calle 8. Computers with internet connections are also available for use within the library.

FPMCQROO *(The Fundación de Parques y Museos de Cozumel de Quintana Roo)*

The *Museo de la Isla*, the *Museo de Navigacion*, *Parque Chankanaab*, and *Parque Sur Eco Park* are all administered by the state organization *FPMCQROO*, or *FPMC*, for short. Their website, **www.fpmcqroo-prensa.blogspot.com** has regular updates (in Spanish) of upcoming events at the parks and museums. You can also visit their other website and **www.cozumelparks.com** for more info. They also offer a credential (for 200 pesos) that will allow residents of the island FREE ACCESS to the museums and parks under their jurisdictions. To get the card, take a copy of your *Residente Visa*, and a copy of your light, water or phone bill to their offices on Juarez at the corner of Av. Pedro Joaquin Coldwell (the building next to the gas station), Monday through Friday between the hours of 8 AM and 4 PM. They will take your photo and you can pick up the card the next day.

Museum of the Island

Museo de la Isla de Cozumel is the local museum. Open daily 9 AM to 5 PM, it is located on the *malecón* at Calle 6 Norte. The museum offers both permanent and temporary exhibits, a library (you do not need to pay the entrance fee to go to the library), and many cultural events during the year.

Entrance fee is 4 dollars, half-price with Cozumel driver's license, or free with a *FPMC* card.

Navigation Museum

Museo de Navigacion is the nautical museum located in the Punta Celerain Lighthouse within the Punta Sur National Park at the south end of the island.

Casa de la Cultura Ixchel

Located on Juarez at Calle 45, the Casa de la Cultura Ixchel offers free concerts, free movies (2nd Wednesday of the month), dance classes (jazz, salsa, ballet, and more), art (drawing, painting, etc.), music lessons (clarinet, classical guitar, etc.), theatre, aerobic dancing, Zumba, Tae Kwon Do, creative writing (in Spanish) and spaces to use for exhibiting art or performances. Although most of the events and classes are directed towards children, many are offered at an adult level. Email them at: **casadelaculturadecozumel@hotmail.com** and ask for a calendar of events and classes.

Punta Sur Eco Park

This park is located at the south end of the island (called Punta Celarain) at kilometer marker 27. The 12 dollar entrance fee (6 dollars for kids 3-11) covers: walk to the top of the lighthouse, entrance to the Museum of Navigation, access to many beaches (some with hammocks, umbrellas and beach chairs), entrance to the observation tower (to watch the birds and crocodiles in Colombia Lagoon), and use of the rest rooms and showers. For an additional fee, you can rent snorkel equipment or kayaks, or eat at one of the two snack bars. The park is open daily, 9 AM to 4 PM. The park is a non-smoking area. Entrance is free with a *FMPC* card. See the website **www.cozumelparks.com**.

City Parks

Besides a number of neighborhood parks equipped with sports fields for soccer, skateboard ramps, playground equipment, and the like, Cozumel has several large sports complexes with tennis courts, running tracks, baseball diamonds, free-weight training, exercise machines, and a swimming pool. These three sports complexes are located at *Unidad Deportiva Bicentenario* at Calle 25 and Av. 65, *Unidad Deportiva Independencia* on Calle 11 Sur between Av. 40 and 50, and *Unidad Deportiva Revolucion* on Av. 95 bis and Calle 12. For more information on their equipment and hours of operation, see the section on **SPORTS.**

DIF

DIF also has a number of parks all over town, and some of them (like the one at Av. Quintana Roo & Av. F.A. Gonzalez Canto) have playground equipment especially designed for handicapped children. Other *DIF* parks offer classes to senior citizens (60 years old and over) in crafts like hammock-making. See the section on **OTHER GOVERNMENT OFFICES** for more info.

San Gervasio Mayan Ruins

The road to San Gervasio Archaeological Park lies 4 miles east of town on the Carretera Transversal. The park lies 5 miles north of the intersection. The best way to see the park is by driving there with your own car or motor-scooter, as the tours can be a little rushed. Be sure and take insect repellent and drinking water. The ruins of the Mayan site of San Gervasio are the highlight of the park and are open to the public (for an entrance fee of 8 dollars) from 8 AM to 4 PM. There are two ticket stands: the first collects a $4 dollar fee that covers the maintenance of the road, parking lot, and park facilities and is run by the *Fundación de Parques y Museos de Cozumel*; the second is run by the *Instituto Nacional de Antropología e Historia (INAH)* and their $4 dollar fee covers the maintenance of the ruins themselves. The park has a snack bar, gift stores, and rest-rooms. Guides are available for hire at the park entrance. Guidebooks (the **Yellow Guide to the Mayan Ruins of San Gervasio**) detailing a self-guided tour and the history of San Gervasio are also on sale on Amazon.com at **https://www.amazon.com/Guide-Mayan-Gevasio-Cozumel-Mexico-ebook/dp/B007RQIYXU/ref=sr_1_12?s=books&ie=UTF8&qid=1482539364&sr=1-12&keywords=ric+hajovsky**

Chankanaab National Park

Located south of town at Kilometer 9 on the *Carretera Costera Sur,* Chankanaab Park offers a wide range of sights and things to do covered under the park's entrance fee, like sea-lion shows, manatee exhibit, dolphin show, eco-archaeological park tour, swimming pool, beach, reefs, showers, bathrooms, beach chairs, hammocks, and huts. For an extra fee, you can also swim with dolphins, have an encounter with a manatee or sea-lion, scuba dive off the beach and view the coral reef there or try it using Snuba or Seatrek hard-hat underwater gear, snorkel, or lay on the beach. No smoking within the park and all snorkelers must use biodegradable sunblock and life vests. No pets allowed. For more info see **www.cozumelparks.com**

National Underwater Park *(Parque Nacional de Arrecifes de Cozumel)*
For more information on *The Parque Nacional de Arrecifes de Cozumel* see the section on **BEACH & OCEAN.**

Chapter 32
CLUBS &
ASSOCIATIONS

Alcoholics Anonymous (AA) In the English AA ROOM, Av. 10 Sur corner of Calle 5 Sur, up the spiral iron staircase, first apartment. Meetings are at 6 PM daily. An open meeting is also held at the Barracuda Hotel at 9 AM on Sunday. See **www.aa-cozumel.org** for more info

Narcotics Anonymous (NA), in English meets Tuesdays and Thursdays at 6 PM at the AA meeting room at Av. 10 Sur corner of Calle 5 Sur, up the spiral iron staircase, first apartment.

Overeaters Anonymous (OA) in English meets Tuesdays and Thursdays at 6 PM at the AA meeting room at Av. 10 Sur corner of Calle 5 Sur, up the spiral iron staircase, first apartment.

Co-Dependents Anonymous (CoDA) and **Al-Anon** meets: Saturdays, at 8 PM on Tuesdays and 4 PM Saturdays in the English AA room, Av. 10 Sur corner of Calle 5 Sur, up the spiral iron staircase, first apartment.

Rotary Club has sessions every Thursday at 9 AM in the office of the harbor pilots on Melgar at Calle 12. phone 872-6400

Masons, Av. 8 de Octubre between Calle 33 & 27, and Av. 15 between Calle Morelos & 3

Obreros del Porvenir #19, Calle 8 between Av. 5 & 10. When contacted, this group told CZM they did not want their phone number or facebook page published.

Chrysalis is a non-profit organization dedicated to providing financial scholastic support for the island's students.
www.barefootincozumel.com/chrys

Friends of Cruz Roja Cozumel
www.cruzrojacozumel.org/friendsoverview

Humane Society of Cozumel is the island's non-profit animal rescue program and clinic/shelter. phone 857-0849; Cell 044-987-800-1897 spca@cozumel.net **www.islacozumel.net/services/spca**

Ciudad de Angeles is a Christian children's home on the island of Cozumel, Mexico. The home accepts young children who have been orphaned, abandoned or abused and gives them a permanent home on the Ciudad de Angeles campus **www.ciudaddeangeles.org**

Fundación Comunitaria Cozumel is a local organization with the goal of promoting programs that provide solutions to the needs of the community and to improve the quality of life of vulnerable groups on the island. **www.fccozumel.org**

Carrie's Heart is a nonprofit 501(c)(3) organization based in Houston, Texas dedicated to improving the education, community involvement and overall quality of life of children with disabilities worldwide **www.carriesheart.org**

Salsa Cozumel Salsa dance club. see **www.salsacozumel.com**

ANSPAC is an organization devoted to self-improvement, located on Av. 8 de Octubre, between calle 29 & 31 Tel/Fax: (987) 872-0338 **anspacozumel@hotmail.com**

Caritas operates a food bank at Av. Andres Q. Roo between Av. 85 bis & Av. 90 (987)-869-2233 **bancocozumel@caritasqr.org**

CityMar, A. C. is an environmentally oriented organization, located on Av. 10 between Calle 3 and Salas

RELIGIOUS ORGANIZATIONS IN COZUMEL

PRESBYTERIAN
Iglesia Presbiteriana de Cozumel, 114-2932, 871-1127
Betel, Calle 100 ÷2 & 4, 115-0674
Eben-Ezer, 30 Av. ÷ 8& 10, 872-1473
El Divino Redentor, Av. Benito Juarez, 116-4420
Luz Divina, 30 Av. ÷17 & 19, 116-4420
Antioquia, Av. Macario Aguilar at 37, 107-9075
Puerta de Esperanza, Carretera Transversal, 113-2613
Tu Eres Mi Refugio, Repobladores, 102-4015
El Buen Pastor, Calle 2 at Av. 120, 115-2210
El Mesías, Calle 3 at Av. 65 Bis, 112-4416
Puerta del Cielo, Calle 21 & 55 ÷ 55 Bis, 130-7455
Emanuel, 90 Av. at Calle 10.

ASSEMBLY OF GOD
El Buen Pastor, 65 Av. Bis & 14 ÷ 16, 101-3858
Príncipe de Paz, 30Av. ÷ 6 & 4,103-8715
Jericolos, Ranchitos, 103-8715
Vida Abundante, 90 Av. ÷ Morelos& Calle 3, 111-7094
Filadelfi, Av. Borges ÷ 7 & Morelos, 100-9000
Peniel, 50 Av ÷ 29 & 31, 107-0351
Fuente de Agua Viva, Calle 7 ÷ 30 & 25 Av., 107-6768
Elohim, Calle 7 ÷ 25 Av. & 30, 102-7645

SEVENTH DAY ADVENTISTS
Maranatha, Calle 33 at Calle 20, 872-2214
80 Av., Av. 80
8 Norte, Calle 8 ÷ Av. 20 & 25
San Gervasio, Av. 85 ÷ Morelos & Calle 5
Central, 10 Av.
KM. 6.0, Carretera Transversal KM 6.0,

PENTECOSTAL
Pentecostal Unida Nacional, Calle 70 ÷ 1 & Salas,105-2558
León de Juda,.45 Av. at 17 Bis
Maranatha, 75 Av. ÷ 4 & 6, 103-0250
Manto Sagrado, Carretera Transversal KM 4.3, 103-1432
Vino Nuevo, 105 Av. ÷ Cl. 2 & 4, 103-3524

Palabra Viva, 65 Bis Av. ÷ Cl. 2 & 4, 101-3460
Seguidores de Jesus, 135 Av.

ROMAN CATHOLIC
Sagrado Corazón de Jesús, Av. 95 Bis ÷ 6 & 8, 869-2014
Nuestra Señora de Guadalupe, Calle 8 at 65 Av., 872-0991
San Miguel, 10 Av. X Juárez, 872-1087
Corpus Cristi, 20 Av. ÷ Cl. 15 & 17, 872-1053
San José del Mar, 40 Av. ÷ Cl. 29 & 31, 857-1539

CHURCH OF CHRIST
Cozumel, 5 Av. & 3 ÷ Rosado Salas, 105-0549
De la Calle 8, Calle ÷ Av. 55 & 55 bis, 564-0671
San Miguel 1, Calle 27 ÷ Av. & Calle 12, 872-7209

OTHERS
El Camino, la Verdad, y la Vida, 85 AV. ÷ 6 & 8, 111-5220
El Camino, la Verdad, y la Vida, Calle 14 at 95 bis, 116-2822
El Camino, La Verdad, y la Vida, Av. 70 at 18
Iglesia de Dios de la Profecía, Calle 27 at 30 AV
Iglesia de Dios de la Profecía, 75 Av., 869-1213
Iglesia de Dios de la Profecía, 105 Av., 119-0678
Apostólica de la Fe en Cristo Jesús, 55 Av ÷ 8 & 10, 114-1948
Apostólica de la Fe en Cristo Jesús, Las Fincas, 103-8706
Ministerio Dejame Ayudarte, 135 Av. at 3, 869-3788
J. C. de Los Santos de los Ultimos Días, Cl. 4 ÷ 35 & 40, 115-8798
Iglesia de Dios, casa de oración, 70 Av. at Calle, 10
1st Bautista Maranatha, 55 Av. ÷ 19 & 21, 112-5468
Convivencia Cristiana Pentecoste, Calle 12 ÷35 & 40, 103-0810
Conferencia Gral de la Iglesia de Dios, Calle 25 ÷14 & 40,114-2622
Iglesia de Dios en México, Av. 95Bis. ÷ 6 & 18, 107-1563
Comunidad Cristiana en México, 30 Av. At 31, 101-8760
Iglesia de Dios, 90 Av. ÷ 12 & 14
La Palabra Hablada, 70 Av. ÷ 2 & 4
Ministerio Jesús es Rey, Cl 39÷Av. 95 & 95Bis, 800-5011
Iglesia de Dios en Cristo Jesús, Calle 33 at Av. 20
Cozumel Community Church, 11 Av. ÷ 15 & 20, 869-3834
Iglesia Alcance Victoria, Calle 12 ÷ 40 & 45, 101-4029
Jesús es el camino, Calle 3 at 95
Iglesia Restauración Elohim, Calle 1 ÷100 & 105, 102-5778

Iglesia Maranatha, Transversal KM 4.5, 101-0501
Ministerios Asociados de Cozumel, 103-0626
Red Mundo Iglesia del Señor Presencia Dios, 35Av. at Cl 1, 118-3016
Congregación Cristiana de los Testigos de Jehová, 65 Av., 103-5628
Congregación Cristiana de los Testigos de Jehová, 30 Av.
Congregación Cristiana de los Testigos de Jehová, Transversal
Dios Vive Columna y Apoyo de la Verdad, Av. Borges ÷ 5&7, 869-6230
Cristianas Pentecostés de la Rep. Mexicana ,70 Av. ÷ 19 & 17, 101-6485
Conquistando Fronteras Cozumel, 60 Av. ÷ 4 & 6, 117-7433
Iglesia Cristiana Independiente, Carretera Transversal KM 2.4
Casa de Oración Centro Cristian El Shadai, Av. Borge, 876-1019
Convivencia Cristiana Pentecostés la Sunamita, 85 AV, 113-8586
Primera Bautista Independiente Maranatha, Cl 1÷130 &135 Av.,120-0831

Jewish
Chabad de Cozumel, upstairs, Plaza del Sol on the plaza, 101-0086

Chapter 33
PHYSICAL FITNESS

Public pool

Unidad Deportiva Independencia has an outdoor Olympic sized pool on Calle 11 Sur between Av. 40 and 50. To get a pool membership you will need to bring:

• 2 infantile size color photos,

• a copy and original of your passport,

• a copy and the original of your *Residente* visa,

• a local doctor's certificate stating that you are in good health

• a blood test, a urine sample, and a stool sample

You also need to pass a swimming test.

The city offers free swim classes that are organized by age and ability, beginning with introduction to swimming for non-swimmers all the way to state and national teams working towards the Olympics. Lap lanes are available on a time-slotted, pre-inscribed manner. To sign up for lap times, see the office at the pool, located at the southeast corner of the facility. Showers and lockers are available, but bring your own lock. Water aerobics classes and open-ocean relay and marathon events are also sponsored by the city. Pool hours are 6 AM to 10 PM. Office hours are 8 AM to 4 PM. Call 869-3045 for more info.

Public tennis courts

Unidad Deportiva Independencia has lighted outdoor tennis courts on Calle 11 Sur between Av. 40 and 50. They are open Monday through

Friday 5 AM to 11 PM and Saturday 6 AM to 11 PM, and Sunday 6 AM to 6 PM with reservations. Courts are also available at *Unidad Deportiva Bicentenario* at Calle 25 and Av. 65.

Exercise equipment and free weights

The city has a well-equipped free weight and exercise machine area that is open the same hours. A $150 peso sign-up fee and $100 pesos a month are required to use the weight an exercise room, but trainers are on hand to give you pointers.

Team sports

The city organizes and trains teams in soccer *(futbol)*, "speed" soccer, basketball, volleyball, track, basketball, softball, judo, windsurfing, wrestling, baseball, handball, weight-lifting, boxing, table tennis, artistic roller-skating, in-line skating, speed skating, and chess. See the office at the northwest corner of the *Unidad Deportiva Independencia* on Calle 11 Sur between Av. 40 and 50.

Running tracks
The city has rubberized running tracks at *Unidad Deportiva Bicentenario* at Calle 25 and Av. 65 and *Unidad Deportiva Independencia* on Calle 11 Sur between Av. 40 and 50.

Basketball courts (6), softball diamonds (2), baseball diamonds (4), soccer fields (11), volleyball courts (3), "speed" soccer fields (3), indoor soccer (1), Multi-use covered courts (4)

The city has fields and courts available at:

Unidad Deportiva Bicentenario at Calle 25 and Av. 65

Unidad Deportiva Independencia on Calle 11 Sur between Av. 40 and 50

Unidad Deportiva Revolución on Av. 95 bis and Calle 12

DIF Unidad Deportiva at Calle 5 between Av. 40 & 50.

Campo de softball Asterio Tejero at Av. 75 at Calle 12

Estadio de Béisbol Rojo Gomez Av. Pedro Joaquin Coldwell at Salas

Campo Futbol Soccer San Gervasio on Av. Magisterio between Morelos and Calle 5

Events

Ironman triathlon
This takes place in November. See **www.ironmancozumel.com** for more info.

The Sacred Mayan Canoe Journey
This is a new tradition, begun in 2007, which celebrates in May the ancient Mayan pilgrimages to Cozumel by canoe from the mainland port of Xcaret. Twenty-five dugout canoes are paddled from the mainland to the island by volunteers in a recreation of the pilgrimage.

Annual Kiteboarding and Windsurfing Tournament
See **www.cozumelkiteboarding.com** for more info.

Swimming marathon and relay races
In February, the city sponsors an open-ocean swimming marathon and relay race. To sign up, see the swim coach at the City pool office at *Unidad Deportiva Independencia* on Calle 11 Sur between Av. 40 and 50. Office hours are 8 AM to 4 PM. Call 869-3045 for more info.

Chapter 34
BEACH & OCEAN

Beach access

The law in Mexico reserves the entire Mexican coastline as a Federal Zone. This zone extends landward 66 feet, 10 inches from the high tide mark. This swath of Federal land is open to the public for their use and enjoyment, 24 hours a day, 7 days a week, 365 days a year.

The exception to this rule are Navy installations, *Administación Portuaria Integral (API)* installations, Caleta Marina, Fonatur Marina, the piers at Punta Langosta, Puerto Maya and the International Pier, the municipal piers and their surrounding areas, municipal, state, and national parks (like Chankanaab and the Eco-park at Punta Sur), and sections of the beach that the government has granted a special concession to the adjoining property owner. These special concessions are usually granted to Hotels, Condo projects, Beach Clubs, Bars and Restaurants by ZOFEMAT, the federal agency in charge of the Federal Zone. Typically, a homeowner with beach-front property does not have a concession, but there are a few cases on the island where they do. However, wherever concessions have been granted, the public has only the right of ACCESS through the concession, and NOT the USE of the beach of the concession without express permission of the concession holder. What all this means is, most of the beaches in Cozumel are open to the public...IF you can find a legal access to the beach and IF it is not under concession or restricted access due to one of the reasons cited above. You can't just walk through someone's property to get to the beach (that is trespassing, a serious crime in Mexico); there has to be some formal, open, public easement to walk or drive through. For more info about the federal zone rules see:
http://207.248.177.25/images/stories/documents/tabasco/14.pdf

Places off-limits to divers, swimmers, and snorkelers

It is illegal for swimmers to come close to the cruise ship piers.

National Maritime Reef Park of Cozumel

In 1996, the *Parque Marino Nacional Arrecifes de Cozumel* was created, in order to protect some of its better reefs and natural underwater areas. The park encompasses 11,000 hectares and includes the beaches and water between Paradise reef and running around the southern end of the island back up to Punta Chiqueros, on the east coast. It is administered jointly by CONAMP (Commission of Protected Natural Areas), *ANOAAT* (Dive Operator's Group), and *SEMARNAT* (Environmental, Natural Resource, and Fishing Secretariat).

The park is patrolled by some very zealous park rangers that enforce the park rules (which are federal law) with zero tolerance for infractions. These rules are:

* Marine organisms in the Park are protected by law

* No fishing or spear-fishing

* No feeding of live organisms;

* No extracting or annoying the marine fauna

* No taking souvenirs (shell collecting)

* No gloves, knives, or spear-guns allowed

* Use only biodegradable sun-blocks and sunscreens

* Oil spills, fuel spills or dumping of garbage is prohibited

* No overnight camping

* No bonfires on the beach

Fishing licenses

Fishing licenses are required for any type of sport fishing (including spear-fishing) in Cozumel's waters. The exception is there is no license needed for fishing from shore with a rod and reel or hand-line. These licenses are available at CONAPESCA/SEGARPA in Playa del Carmen at the corner of 1st street south and 20 avenue on the second floor. Their phone number is 984) 803-9726. Licenses for non-citizens are 127 pesos a day, 318 pesos per week, 476 pesos per month, or 635 pesos per year. The license is good anywhere in Mexico. If you are caught fishing without a license, you may be hit with a hefty fine and your equipment confiscated. Capturing fish live for removal to an aquarium is prohibited. Catch and release is encouraged.

The sport fishing bag limits are: No more than 10 fish per day, including no more than 5 of any single species, except marlin, sailfish, swordfish and shark, of which only one specimen from this group is allowed, and which counts 5 towards the overall 10 fish daily limit. A dorado, roosterfish, shad, or tarpon each count as 5 towards the overall 10 fish daily limit, and only 2 fish can be kept daily from this group. Only one rod per person is allowed. Spear fishing is only allowed while skin diving without scuba tanks, and there is a 5 fish daily limit for spear-fishermen. Only rubber-band or spring type harpoons are allowed. No mollusks or crustaceans (including crab, conch, and lobster) may be taken with a sport fishing license. It is illegal to sell fish taken with a sport fishing license. Fish taken may not be filleted aboard. Licenses may be purchased by the day, week, month, or year. Fees range from $12.40 to $67.00

Protected aquatic species

The taking of conch from any water adjacent to Cozumel is strictly prohibited, as is the taking of any species of sea-turtle or their eggs. The taking of any species of marine mammals are likewise prohibited. Snorkeling with the protected whale-shark is only allowed with organized tours that have a special permit.

Chapter 35
METRIC CONVERSION TABLES

Mexico uses the metric system of measurement. If you are not accustomed to using it, it can be a little trying at times. If you have a hard time converting kilograms, kilometers and kilopascals in your head, just refer to the following conversion tables. And remember, the speed limits posted are in kilometers per hour, not miles per hour, and the traffic police have already heard that excuse many times, so don't try it!

Air pressure

Your automobile's tire air pressure is expressed in kilopascals in Mexico. Multiply the pound force per square inch (psi) by 6.89 to get kilopascals (kPa)
24 psi = 165 kPa
26 psi = 179 kPa
28 psi = 193 kPa
30 psi = 207 kPa
32 psi = 221 kPa
34 psi = 235 kPa

To find the US dollar cost per gallon of your car's gas:

1. Multiply the number of liters pumped by 0.26 and that will give you the number of gallons pumped.
2. Divide the total cost of the gas in pesos by your exchange rate (12.5, etc.), and that will give you the total cost in US dollars.

3. Divide the total cost of the gas in US dollars by the number of gallons pumped and that will give you the US dollar cost per gallon.

Weight measure

To get grams, multiply the number of ounces by 28.349
To get kilograms, multiply the number of pounds by 0.454
To get ounces, multiply grams by 0.035
To get pounds, multiply kilograms by 2.205

Liquid measure

1 fluid ounce (oz) = 29.57 milliliters (ml)
1 pint (pt) = 0.47 liters (lt)
1 quart (qt) = 0.946 liters (lt)
1 gallon (gl) = 3.785 liters (lt)

Gallons to Liters
1 = 3.78
2 = 7.57
3 = 11.35
4 = 15.14
5 = 18.92
6 = 22.71
7= 26.49
8 = 30.28
9 = 34.06
10 = 37.85
15 = 56.78
20 = 75.70
25 = 94.63
30 = 113.56

Liters to Gallons

1 = 0.26
2 = 0.53
3 = 0.79
4 = 1.06
5 = 1.32
6 = 1.59
7 = 1.85
8 = 2.11
9 = 2.38
10 = 2.64
15 = 3.96
20 = 5.28
25 = 6.60
30 = 7.93

Area measure

1 hectare = 2.471 acres
1 metro cuadrado = 10.764 sq. ft.

Linear measure

1 inch = 2.54 centimeters (cm)
1 foot = 30.48 centímetros (cm)
1 yard = 0.91 metros (m)
1 mile = 1.61 kilómetros (km)
1 milímetro =.03937 inches
1 centímetro = .3937 inches
1 metro= 39.37 inches
1 kilometer = .621 miles
1 braza = 6 feet
1 vara = 16.5 feet
1 legua = 3 miles

Volume
1 centímetro cubico = .061 cubic inches
1 metro cubico (estério) = 1.3 cubic yds.

Approximations
1 kilometer is about 5/8 of a mile, or about 0.62 miles.
To make a rough conversion of kilometers into miles, multiply kilometers by 1.6

Kilometers to Miles to Kilometers
1 Kilometer (km) equals 0.62 Miles (mi)
1 Mile (mi) equals 1.6 Kilometers (km)

kilometers = miles
1 = 0.62
2 = 1.24
3 = 1.86
4 = 2.48
5 = 3.10
6 = 3.72
7 = 4.34
8 = 4.97
9 = 5.59
10 = 6.21
11 = 6.83
12 = 7.45
13 = 8.07
14 = 8.69
15 = 9.32
16 = 9.94
17 = 10.56
18 = 11.18
19 = 11.80
20 = 12.42

21 = 13.04
22 = 13.67
23 = 14.29
24 = 14.91
25 = 15.53
26 = 16.15
27 = 16.77
28 = 17.39
29 = 18.01
30 = 18.64
31 = 19.26
32 = 19.88
33 = 20.50
34 = 21.12
35 = 21.74
36 = 22.36
37 = 22.39
38 = 23.61
39 = 24.23
40 = 24.85
41 = 25.47
42 = 26.09
43 = 26.71
44 = 27.34
45 = 27.96
46 = 28.58
47 = 29.20
48 = 29.82
49 = 30.44
50 = 31.06
60 = 37.28
70 = 43.49
80 = 49.70
90 = 55.92

100 = 62.10
200 = 124.2
300 = 186.4
400 = 248.5
500 = 310.6
1,000 = 621.3

miles = kilometers

1 = 1.60
2 = 3.21
3 = 4.82
4 = 6.43
5 = 8.04
6 = 9.65
7 = 11.26
8 = 12.87
9 = 14.48
10 = 16.09
11 = 17.7
12 = 19.3
13 = 20.9
14 = 22.5
15 = 24.1
16 = 25.7
17 = 27.4
18 = 29.0
19 = 30.6
20 = 32.2
21 = 33.8
22 = 35.4
23 = 37.0
24 = 38.6
25 = 40.2
26 = 41.8

27 = 43.5
28 = 45.1
29 = 46.7
30 = 48.3
31 = 49.9
32 = 51.5
33 = 53.1
34 = 54.7
35 = 56.3
36 = 57.9
37 = 59.5
38 = 61.2
39 = 62.8
40 = 64.4
41 = 66.0
42 = 67.6
43 = 69.2
44 = 70.8
45 = 72.4
46 = 74.0
47 = 75.6
48 = 77.2
49 = 78.8
50 = 80.5
60 = 96.6
70 = 112.7
80 = 128.7
90 = 144.8
10 = 160.9
200 = 321.9
300 = 482.8
400 = 643.7
500 = 804.6
1,000 = 1,609.3

degrees Celsius °C	-40	-20	0	20	37	60	80	100
°F	-40		0	32	80	98.6	160	212
degrees Fahrenheit						body temperature		water boils

To convert Fahrenheit to Celsius
Subtract 32 from Fahrenheit temperature, multiply by 5, and divide by 9

To convert Celsius to Fahrenheit
Multiply the Celsius temperature by 9, divide by 5, and add 32

Cooking
1 taza (cup) = 8 fl ounces = 16 cucharadas (table spoons) = 48 cucharaditas (teaspoons)

Do not forget, the temperatures marked on ovens and stoves in Mexico a marked in Celsius, and NOT Fahrenheit!

ABOUT THE AUTHOR

Ric Hajovsky and his wife, Marie-France Lemire, own CZM, S. de R. L. de C. V., a Cozumel marketing and publishing company that produces maps and guides like *The Free Yellow Map of Cozumel.*

www.EverythingCozumel.com is CZM's website, and it holds a wealth of information about the island. It is a must read for anyone contemplating a visit.

Other books and eBooks Ric has written include:

The True History of Cozumel

The Lost Kivas of San Lazaro

The Yellow Guide to the Mayan Ruins of San Gervasio

Xcaret, The surprising history found underneath this Mexican theme park

Tulum: Everything you need to know before you go the ruins

December 21, 2012:Everything you need to know to understand what all the fuss is about

The History of Horseshoes

The True & Faithful Account of the Adventures of Trader Ric
    Part I: in Kuna Yala
    Part II: on the trail of Cristobal Colon
    Part III: at the headwaters of the Tapanahonie
    Part IV: in the Darien Gap

Spain: Hidden Secrets & Dirty Tricks; how to travel in Spain in high style, but at a budget price.

You Can't Get There From Here!

¡Vale!

Made in the USA
Columbia, SC
13 September 2022

67053614R10102